# REVOLUTIONARY
# INTEGRATION
## A Marxist Analysis of African American Liberation

# REVOLUTIONARY INTEGRATION

A Marxist Analysis of African American Liberation

## by Richard Fraser and Tom Boot

Introduction by Guerry Hoddersen

RED LETTER PRESS
Seattle

© 2004 by Red Letter Press
4710 University Way NE, Suite 100
Seattle, WA 98105 • (206) 985-4621
RedLetterPress@juno.com
www.RedLetterPress.org
Printed in the United States of America

Revised Edition 2004

Cover photo by Declan Haun, 1961
Back cover illustration by William Siegel, 1939
Cover designs by Anya Willow

Library of Congress Cataloging-in-Publication Data

Fraser, Richard S., 1913-1988.
    Revolutionary integration : a Marxist analysis of African
American liberation / by Richard Fraser and Tom Boot ;
introduction by Guerry Hoddersen.– Rev. ed.
    p. cm.
    First issued as two separate works. Revolutionary integration :
the dialectics of Black liberation was published as an internal
bulletin of the Socialist Workers Party in 1963. A revised ed.
appeared in two installments of the Freedom Socialist newspaper, vol. 3, nos. 3 and 4 (fall and winter 1977). Revolutionary
integration : yesterday and today was adopted by the Freedom
Socialist Party in 1982 and was published in the Freedom
Socialist, vol. 8, no. 2 (spring 1983).
    Includes bibliographical references and index.
    ISBN 0-932323-22-7
    1. African Americans–Civil rights–History–20th century.
2. Civil rights movements–United States–History–20th century.
3. African Americans–Race identity. 4. Black power–United
States–History–20th Century. 5 African Americans–Politics and
government–20th century. 6. African American women–
Political activity–History–20th century. 7. Socialism–United
States–History–20th century. 8. Freedom Socialist Party (U.S.)
9. Socialist Workers Party. 10. United States–Race relations–
Political aspects. I. Boot, Tom, 1949- II. Title.

E185.615.F725 2003
323.1196′073′009–dc22
                                                        2003058796

# Contents

INTRODUCTION TO THE 2004 EDITION
by Guerry Hoddersen    9

## 1. Dialectics of Black Liberation

PREFACE    15

THE COMING SOUTHERN REVOLUTION    20
The southern police state    20
The role of the government in the South    22
Federal troops to the South    23
The southern labor party    26
The strategic power of northern labor    27

THE NORTH: PROLONGED CRISIS OF
LEADERSHIP AND QUEST FOR A PROGRAM    30
The reformist leadership    30
The nationalist alternative to reformism    33
Racial segregation: A unique oppression    37
The race question and the National Question    38
Black separatism    41
The Black nationalism of white radicals    49
Separatism and the freedom struggle    55

THE BLACK MOVEMENT    56
The impact of Black culture on American society    57
A vanguard of the class struggle    61
Blacks and independent politics    64

THE REVOLUTIONARY MARXIST PARTY
IN THE BLACK STRUGGLE    68
The record    68
The source    78
The future    83

# 2. Revolutionary Integration: Yesterday and Today

OVERVIEW    91
Premises    92
The present conjuncture    93

THE COMINTERN ADDRESSES THE BLACK QUESTION    95
A special question    97
The Second Congress, 1920    98
The Fourth Congress, 1922    100

LENIN ON THE NATIONAL/COLONIAL QUESTION    101

STALIN'S BLACK BELT DICTUM    104

DEBATE IN THE FOURTH INTERNATIONAL    107
The Trotsky-Swabeck discussion, 1933    108
The Trotsky-Johnson discussion, 1939    111
The 1939 resolution    112
SWP campaigns for equality    115
The 1948 resolution    121

EMERGENCE OF THE REVOLUTIONARY
INTEGRATION POSITION    123
1957: A blessing on Rev. King    127
Showdown at the 1963 convention    128
SWP: The aftermath    130

REVOLUTIONARY INTEGRATION
IN THE TURBULENT 1960s    133
The Black reformists    134
The Black radicals    136
Impact of Blacks on labor    147
Twilight    155

THE 1970s: CULTURAL NATIONALISM
AND BLACK MACHO    156

REBIRTH AND RETREAT OF BLACK FEMINISM    161
The isolation of Black feminists    162

Socialist feminism 165
Black lesbians and gay men 166
The road ahead 171

## THE 1980S: THE BLACK MOVEMENT
## IN THE REAGAN ERA 172
Misery and terror for the Black community 172
The Black struggle and the Left 173
Striking a blow for global freedom 191
Black revolt and Permanent Revolution 193

## WHAT MUST BE DONE 195
Our general course 196
Emphasize the leadership role of Black
women and Black lesbians and gays 197
United front and multi-issue work 199
Organize for a labor party 199
Slogans for the struggle 200

## AFTERWORD 201


**NOTES** 203
**INDEX** 215

# Images of Black Liberation
## Photographs

Birmingham, AL civil rights demonstration, 1963    21

Troops occupy the University of Mississippi, 1962    25

Claude McKay addresses the Comintern, 1922    35

Marcus Garvey    45

Elijah Muhammad    45

"Street Life—Harlem"    59

Ella Baker and Fanny Lou Hamer    65

Socialist Workers Party graphic, 1945    74

C.L.R. James    80

Malcolm X    86

Meeting for Black and white labor solidarity, 1935    96

Campaign to free the Scottsboro Boys    106

Black nurses in WWII    115

Memphis sanitation workers strike, 1968    125

Montgomery, Alabama bus boycott    135

Philadelphia Black Panther Party rally, 1970    143

March on Washington for Jobs and Freedom, 1963    149

Michele Wallace    158

Black contingent at Lesbian/Gay March on Washington    167

Workers World Party campaign brochure, 1984    176

Stokely Carmichael    184

"White and Black Unite"    195

# Introduction to the 2004 Edition

In 1965, when I was 20 years old, I worked in rural Mississippi for the Student Nonviolent Coordinating Committee (SNCC), registering Black voters and attempting to desegregate public facilities. That experience changed my life. What I saw there made me rethink what I thought I knew about my country. Southern poverty—Black, white and Native American—left a deep impression. It seemed so deliberate, so fundamental to the South and so useful to the North. White violence and racial hatred stood in stark contrast to the bravery of workingclass African American women and men like Mr. and Mrs. Hill of Carthage, Mississippi, with whose family I lived during my short stint in the Deep South.

In later years, when people asked me why I became a radical and a socialist, I would say they could blame it on the Magnolia State. But that wasn't the whole story.

From Mississippi, I returned to school at the University of California at Berkeley with more questions than answers. I was disturbed by the competition among civil rights organizations and the NAACP's sabotage of SNCC initiatives. I was dismayed by disputes between civil rights and Black liberation leaders over separatism vs. integration; the proper role of whites in the movement (if there was one); sexism and the secondary status accorded most women; and the usefulness of pacifism in the face of unbridled official violence. Most important, to my mind, was the question of how to unseat the white oligarchy that still ruled the South and had moved into the White House with Lyndon Johnson's ascension to the presidency.

Despite the courage, the deaths and the immense sacrifices of civil rights fighters, continuing long after I left Mississippi, the American apartheid system was still intact. Legal reforms, while important, had not eliminated the South's institutionalized racism, anti-unionism and race/caste/class divisions. For a couple of years, I tried not to think about all this because it was so depressing. Instead, I worked in the anti-Vietnam War movement and the early feminist struggle, and helped defend the Black Panthers in Oakland.

Then I read the first half of the book you hold in your hands. It was then a mimeographed paper entitled "Revolutionary Integration: The Dialectics of Black Liberation." It had been researched and formulated by a minority Socialist Workers Party tendency led by Richard Fraser (Kirk) and Clara Fraser (Kaye) and submitted as a resolution to the party's 1963 convention. ("Kirk" and "Kaye" were political pseudonyms adopted by the Frasers because of the intense harassment of radicals during the McCarthy period.)

I will never forget the excitement with which I read the section outlining a strategy for the southern struggle. In response to the lawless brutality of white Mississippi, it fashioned an eminently sensible, completely revolutionary program that was based on U.S. history, Marxist economics, union experience, and Black radical scholarship.

These words hit me like a ton of bricks: *"Central to the southern struggle is the demand upon Congress that southern congressmen be denied their seats on the grounds that they do not represent legal state governments but a regime imposed after violent overthrow of legal authority and maintained for nearly a century by force and violence... All armed forces under the jurisdiction of present state governments, including local police and sheriffs' bodies, shall be disbanded and disarmed. A volunteer militia shall be recruited from amongst those who support the U.S. Constitution. Governments shall be formed under author-ity of Congress and supervision of the militias on the basis of universal suffrage of all persons over 18 years of age."*

These were ideas with the power to transform the con-sciousness of whites, Blacks and all oppressed peoples, North and South, and to mobilize a national movement for fundamental political change in the U.S.

The primary education Mississippi had given me was completed by the ideas of Revolutionary Integration: that racism was the *prerequisite* for capitalism's establishment in our hemisphere and, just like sexism, is necessary for its continued rule; that the demand for racial justice and in-tegration (not assimilation or separatism) produces a politi-cal upheaval that is transitional to socialism and creates a revolutionary Black vanguard; that the fight against racism must become anti-capitalist if it is to make economic and social gains for the *masses* and not just a handful of entre-preneurs and opportunists.

Some 30 years later, these ideas still strike me as a brilliant analysis of that turbulent period. Many fine books have been written that tell the story of the civil rights effort from the viewpoint of local movements and organizers. Readers now can find critical evaluations of issues initially only addressed in "Dialectics of Black Liberation": the role of the established civil rights organizations, southern white business, the Black Muslims, reformist preachers, southern Democrats, sexist males, and Presidents Johnson and Kennedy. But none of these books attempt to lay out a strategy for a movement capable of inspiring African

American trade unionists, breaking northern labor out of its passivity, defending the key leadership of grassroots female civil rights organizers, and winning Black freedom as part of a broad revolt against capitalism and for socialism. *Revolutionary Integration* tells the history, but it is more than a history book. It is a handbook for revolutionaries.

It is a tragedy that the SWP had already begun its slide into conservatism and bureaucracy by the time this resolution was written. SWP leaders would not permit a democratic discussion of Revolutionary Integration and its criticisms of both the civil rights reformists and the virulently anti-female and abstentionist Black Muslims. The dissident tendency was told, in essence, to shut up or get out.

Refusing to stifle their views on this and other issues, Richard Fraser, Clara Fraser and the entire Seattle branch left the SWP and founded the Freedom Socialist Party (FSP) in 1965. Revolutionary Integration became one of the party's main theoretical pillars.

Seventeen years later, the second half of this book, "Revolutionary Integration: Yesterday and Today," was written by Tom Boot on behalf of the FSP National Committee and adopted by the 1982 party convention.

This section takes off where "The Dialectics of Black Liberation" ended: with the Black movement of 1963 poised to move in a revolutionary direction against the southern police state, but lacking a leadership with a viable theory and bold perspective. Boot examines the contenders for radical Black leadership between 1963 and 1982, taking a special look at Malcolm X, Robert Williams, the Black Panther Party, SNCC, and the League of Revolutionary Black Workers. He retraces the contribution made by leaders of the Russian Revolution in insisting that U.S. socialists shake off their own prejudices, pay attention to the problems of Blacks and champion their cause. He dissects the destructive role played by the Communist Party in directing African Americans into the Democratic Party and by the SWP, which tail-ended first reformism and then Black separatism. He examines the faulty premise that Black capitalism is an antidote to the powerlessness of Black workers and takes a hard look at the destructive influence of sexism and heterosexism, especially within the African American community and the Left.

Finally, Boot brings it all together in a synthesis of Black history and culture, Marxism, women's rights, and gay liberation known as socialist feminism. This optimistic perspective is the unique contribution to U.S. radicalism made by the Freedom Socialist Party and its sister organization, Radical Women.

Some may question how optimism is possible when 30% of all African American children still live in poverty (a rate *double* the national average); when the suicide rate for Black 10-to-14-year-olds increased 223% between 1980-1995; when two-thirds of the 100,000 youth in detention are children of color; when the non-union South is the fastest-growing economic region and still rules the legislative agenda in Congress and the outcome in presidential elections. But what is the alternative? Cynicism is a comfortable resting place for the discouraged and the privileged. The rest of us must keep faith with those that went before, learn from their mistakes, and press on.

Reading this book will make you mad about missed opportunities. It will make you think about the future. And it will make you want to join the perpetual, international struggle for "Freedom Now!" which is still very much on the agenda in the U.S. and around the world. As my Southern mother used to say, "Those who were not born to live in the world as it is were born to change it." And we will.

GUERRY HODDERSEN
Seattle, Washington

# 1. Dialectics of Black Liberation

*This document originally appeared as a resolution submitted to the 1963 national convention of the Socialist Workers Party (SWP) by Richard Fraser, and his co-thinkers in the SWP. The Revolutionary Integration tendency included all the members of the SWP's Seattle branch, who left that party in 1966 and formed the Freedom Socialist Party (FSP). The FSP adopted Revolutionary Integration as one of its founding principles.*

## Preface

The Black revolt in the southern U.S.A. stands objectively on the threshold of a new stage in its development: a stage of political organization for revolution, involving a showdown struggle *against* the southern police state and *for* a new democratic political system.

Southern Black militants, young and old, have sustained a courageous struggle for the past ten years. After the high points of Montgomery[1] (where workingclass leaders pushed the ministers into the foreground) and Little Rock[2] (officially led by the National Association for the Advancement of Colored People while an armed community waited), the movement tended to recede.

Restless over the inaction of the clergy and NAACP, Black youth entered the scene, bringing struggles to life all over the South. Sometimes with small numbers, but with indomitable spirit, they catapulted the morale of the movement and shamed their elders into motion.

The movement as a whole operated generally within the confines of reformism—the attempt to change the racial climate of the South by reform. While the youth in Student Nonviolent Coordinating Committee (SNCC)[3] never considered themselves bound to reformism in principle and are politically unprejudiced and open-minded, they have not challenged the *theory* of reformism.

The Robert Williams movement in Monroe did.[4] It synthesized the activism of the youth, the proletarian ranks and behind-the-scenes worker leadership of Montgomery, and the mass aggressiveness later displayed so dramatically in Birmingham.[5] Williams was the first to publicly project a radical ideology, a bold and revolutionary strategy, and a proud internationalism.

The three streams of the civil rights movement—youth, the church, and the working masses—converged in Birmingham, with the ministers fronting. Birmingham was to be the culminating effort, the key battle of the ten-year struggle to break the back of segregation in the South.

The civil rights activists fought heroically. They shook the country and the world. They emerged with honor and with new strength—but with no concessions. All agreements made by the Birmingham petty-bourgeoisie were nullified by the overwhelming pressure of the southern police state.

For the participants, this only confirms what they already know or feel—that there is no possibility of winning Freedom Now through pressure-attempts to reform the totalitarian police state.

The preachers placed ultimate faith in the federal government, which had failed in all of its promises, and here failed again. President Kennedy's man in Birmingham failed miserably in his "arbitration" operation and the Brothers Kennedy stood glaringly exposed as fakers. The Reverends, in turn, lost much prestige in the process.

And who gained stature? Robert Williams. A figure like Leroi Jones,[6] a *northern* intellectual in Birmingham as a reporter, assured his audiences of street demonstrators that their experiences proved the validity of the concepts of Robert Williams.

Birmingham represented the failure and exposure of reformism in the South, but it simultaneously represented a great leap forward in organization, experience and awareness. The mood, the pace, the tremendous dynamic of the demonstrations are reminiscent of great strikes and insurrections. Observers and participants are tremendously stirred by the complex phenomenon they witnessed: an elated but still disappointed community soberly evaluating its overwhelming experience.

The militant Blacks of the South are now groping for the handle of a new weapon. They know or sense what it is, but they hesitate to articulate it. The essence of it is:

•There must be a new leadership, radical and bold.

•The leaders must be prepared to lead a revolution, because the whole police state system must be destroyed.

• A political struggle, requiring a new political party, is the only vehicle for basic change.

Being a one-to-four minority in the South, however, dims the prospect of Blacks overthrowing the police state alone. Consequently, they will realize that they must so fashion their strategy as to break through the racist wall separating them from the white workers and poor farmers, and assert the identity of political interest and the common class interest which cross the color line. Together, they will forge a merged struggle for democratic rights—for race equality, civil liberties and the rights of labor.

As it develops its revolutionary perspective, the southern civil rights movement will orient toward an alliance with a revived northern labor movement. Only northern labor has the power to paralyze the ability of the government to intervene against the southern revolution. And since the southern Black movement cannot wait until northern labor sheds its passivity and bureaucratic leadership, it must proceed to shake up and spur northern labor into life.

Southern Blacks will thus profoundly stimulate the northern giant into recovering its capacity for struggle.

•   •   •

Geographically separated, facing two complementary but different forms of capitalist rule, and responding with diverse tactics and levels of consciousness, the southern movement and the movement "Up South" and West are still bound together by mutual experiences, solidarity, and exploding racial consciousness born of frustration too long endured.

Militant currents emerging from the seething ghettos of the North and West recognize the blind alley of reformism. Ignored by the labor bureaucracy, and suspicious or uncertain of the ability of socialist organizations to understand and/or adapt to the needs of the Black struggle, these militants long have been grappling with the problem of the *nationwide crisis of leadership in the movement.*

As a consequence of this crisis, they are experimenting with local and regional levers of upsetting the status quo, and are prepared for more massive and radical assaults upon white supremacy as conditions ripen.

The vacuum produced by the long hiatus of the reformist leaders found poignant expression in the rise of the Black Muslims. As a fiery propaganda sect, they spurred the reformist leaders by unmasking their accommodation to white domination and by agitating the entire country with pithy truths about race relations in the United States.

The doctrine of separatism, however, orients this movement away from the physical struggle against racial discrimination into contemptuous abstentionism. The Muslims substitute for combat a classic utopian attempt to build an independent Black economy in the United States.

The Muslim movement is a contradiction: articulate and defiant, but superstitious and backward. It is a transitional phenomenon which will cease to exert its appeal when a more rational and internally consistent movement develops in the Black community to fulfill the demand for truth, audacity, a goal, and uncorrupted leadership.

From where will this leadership emerge?

The Black movement in the North is extremely complex and its dynamics invariably produce a multitude of leadership sources. A number of militant, race conscious, independent and determined organizations have already appeared in northern cities, headed by new, younger leaders who are developing swiftly and might well become part of the future national leadership.

The impact of the southern struggle is stirring vast new layers, especially the broad church section.

Many older militants and independent radicals are invigorated by events and ready for action.

A new powerful force among artists and intellectuals is heralded by the appearance of individuals like writer James Baldwin, journalist William Worthy, playwright Lorraine Hansberry, and others.

Northern Blacks have been ready for a basic social change for decades, and we should expect to find new leadership from every walk of life, every institution, every city, every class! Above all, as the revolutionary perspective is increasingly projected, the relatively privileged Black trade unionists will again come boldly forward.

•   •   •

The accelerating Black Revolt represents the most significant revolutionary development of our time, the most fertile field for the growth and flowering of socialist ideas, the most dynamic spur to the working class as a whole and the finest source of new radical leadership.

A revolutionary Marxist party must be oriented to take advantage of the opportunities this situation offers. Given solid ideological footing, sensitivity and flexibility, such a party can make giant strides in unison with the Black movement.

# The coming southern revolution

### The southern police state

In Birmingham, the reformist program came to the end of the line.

Day and night, wave after wave of children, youth and adults asserted the right to public prayer—a most elementary form of the right of assemblage. Masses of Blacks fought a sustained, largely nonviolent civil war for days, paralyzing the city, filling its jails, destroying its trade and reducing its industrial production.

A few reforms were conceded by local businessmen, but within two days the agreement evaporated. It was revealed to anybody who didn't already know it that the white businessmen had no authority to limit segregation because the true political authority is the White Citizens Council and the Klan. Police, politicians and businessmen belong to and take orders from these bodies.

The whole arsenal of passive resistance was lined up against the police state. It didn't work. The bruised and injured demonstrators returned from battle and jail with a huge moral victory—but no concrete gains.

The totalitarian character of the police state of the South was clearly unmasked—its immovable resistance to change, and its inability to concede even modest reforms, despite legal action, passive resistance, love, militant mass action and sporadic violence. Most Blacks in the South recognize, in essence, the existence of a police state. But now it has been exposed in a giant struggle, after preliminary skirmishes and testing in Montgomery, Albany, Monroe, and hundreds of other cities and towns.

Modern capitalist rule basically takes form in either bourgeois democracy or fascism; various levels and combinations of police and military dictatorships serve as transitions. When a state cannot both protect capital and win public acceptance, it must smash all official channels of political expression and resort nakedly to its repressive forces. Such a state will immediately use these forces at the first sign of a mere difference with its policies.

Such a state is a *police state,* not just quantitatively but

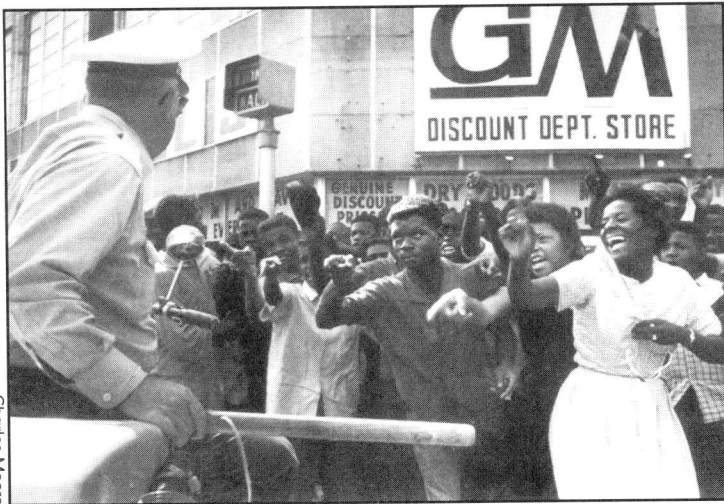

Charles Moore

*Birmingham youth celebrate a brief victory in May 1963. By challenging white supremacy, African Americans took on the southern police state in a social upheaval that had the potential to ignite a revolution.*

qualitatively different than the democratic form of rule.

The southern state provides no legal channels whatever for the democratic process, however strong the democratic movement may be. Even for southern white workers, there is no meaning in the right to vote and no real freedom of speech, assemblage or press. Elections are plebiscites, as under Hitler and Mussolini. Union organizing is virtually impossible.

The southern regime freezes all social relations in the rigid mold of legal racism, wherein every action and thought must conform to the diseased mores of white supremacy and segregation.

The regime is not only a totalitarian police state, it encompasses definite characteristics of fascism, i.e., support by a mass middleclass base. But this base is so badly deteriorated that the state can be described only as *"fascist-like,"* in recognition of its retention of some portion of mass support capable of terrorism.

Writer Truman Nelson's description of the emerging consciousness of this phenomenon is to the point: "There is a recognition (by Blacks) that municipal government there is a military one along the lines of troops occupying and controlling an enemy or colonial people."

The lesson of Birmingham is that even mass actions which bring the businessmen and police to their knees are not enough. *The enemy is an entrenched, fascist-like, police state system.*

## The role of the government in the South

Nelson calls the South a "lunatic society" and despairs of anything short of coercion by the North to effect any change.

Will the United States government initiate or force enough reform to align southern discrimination with the level of legal equality in the North and West?

Hardly. The capitalist class, its political parties, and its machinery of state helped to create the totalitarian racist regime of the South nearly a century ago, in order to crush the democratic alliance of the Freedmen and the white farmers during Reconstruction. United States capital then incorporated this new dictatorship into its national economic, political and social organization.

Today, far from being inclined to release anew the revolutionary energy of the southern working class, capitalism instead prepares to resort to a police state in the North.

Present trends toward fascist development (like the Hargis-Walker duet[7]) indicate that the obvious road for U.S. capitalism, as the general crisis deepens, is the nationwide extension of the southern system, rather than vice-versa.

Short of all-out fascism, the political stability of capitalist rule must rest in large measure upon the continued disenfranchisement of the southern working class, both Black and white. The solid and never changing reactionary southern bloc that dominates Congress has provided the formula for the two-party system since 1876, and the present United States political structure could not survive without its southern pole.

On the one hand, the bloc exercises a chronically retrogressive veto power, an extra-legal check added on to the check-and-balance system. On the other hand, the bloc facilitates survival of demagogic northern liberalism by undertaking a constant parliamentary sham battle. In Congress, the Bill of Rights, the antislavery amendments, and human dignity are stage-props for both sides.

"Senator," says the Congressman from the Deep South to the northern liberal, "let me know if you are ever in trouble. I'll attack you."

## Federal troops to the South

To obscure the basic dependence of the government upon the southern system, to create the illusion that the government desires and will effect drastic changes in the South, and to project a democratic image for international consumption, the government rattles the sword at the Bourbon South and even sends troops, ostensibly to rescue a few Blacks in distress.

What is the actual function of the troops?

*To prevent self-defense.* Eisenhower only dispatched troops to Little Rock at the mayor's insistence that the Black community was an armed camp prepared to slaughter the headstrong Klan.

Kennedy developed an ominous new theme during the Birmingham crisis. Not only did he send troops to Alabama only *after* the Blacks had gained the initiative and whipped the Birmingham police and fire departments, but he justified their continued presence by citing the "danger" from "extremists"—from both sides, of course. Blacks have a pretty good idea of which "extremists" will take the beating from federal troops.

*To help racist politicians.* Kennedy's fantastic invasion of the University of Mississippi with huge armies, out of all proportion to the need for James Meredith's safety, [8] was designed to prevent a split in the white community.

The town of Oxford, threatened with removal of accredited academic status for the University of Mississippi as a consequence of Governor Ross Barnett's interference, was prepared to accept Meredith as an alternative to the expected exodus of students. Kennedy's troops offset the emergence of a conflict among whites over Barnett, and held intact the authority and power of the state officials by allowing them to be defeated by an overwhelming *outside* force instead of local opposition.

*To improve the United States image.* Kennedy used troops in "Ole Miss" to enhance the image of the United States government for international consumption, projecting the government as a champion of democracy even in

Charles Moore

*On October 1, 1962, President Kennedy mobilized 30,000 federal marshals, national guardsmen, and army troops in response to riots protesting the enrollment of the University of Mississippi's first Black student, James Meredith.*

the face of solid racist public opinion. It is highly probable, also, that the mock battle with Barnett was staged with the idea in mind of mollifying world opinion in advance of the forthcoming invasion of Cuba.

*To intimidate the working class.* The University of Mississippi spectacle, displaying the massive, ready, arbitrary and ruthless power of the government to handle domestic conflicts, produced a bulldozing effect on workers.

*For the record.* Eisenhower used his Little Rock troops operation as a smokescreen for a drastic retreat on the civil rights front. The White House will not change the South, and the way federal troops are used divulges this clearly enough.

The administration, however, will take enough steps to mollify Roy Wilkins and Co.[9] and secure their allegiance for another season.

Any gains engineered by the White House will be pure tokens of temporary character gilded with big future promises. Assistance to Blacks will be granted only to keep the southern system basically intact, and to forestall and slow down the struggle. Neither international pressure nor threats of domestic insurrection will budge the federal government into rearranging the basic pattern of southern totalitarianism.

## The southern labor party

If the southern police state is so constructed as to preclude meaningful change, and if the federal government is not going to intervene decisively for social reform, the only road left for achieving civil rights is the political revolution, wherein the racist, oligarchy is destroyed and the people take the power directly into their own hands.

Indeed, such action would constitute a very *legal* revolution, merely seeking to return constitutional law to the South. The present lawless regime overthrew by force and violence the democratically selected governments of the Reconstruction, and has ruled for nearly a century by force and violence, in complete defiance of the Constitution.

But legal or not, a revolution is an enormous undertaking, and as the radicalism of the southern movement evolves, its logical strategy would comprise two main features:

1. The Black minority in the South needs allies.

2. The political struggle requires a political party as an ideological-organizational center and lever.

Average southern white workers are doomed to poverty and degradation until they are able to identify with Blacks, the symbol of southern labor whose degradation reflects on all labor. Inasmuch as the Black movement holds the initiative and will probably continue to hold it, upon it devolves the responsibility for encouraging the white workers to join a common struggle against the police state and jointly build a political party as the instrument of struggle.

A southern labor party is the only kind of organism which embodies the needs of class unity this side of socialism. Whatever it may be named, the construction of a political party serving the interests of Blacks and white workers is the next stage of development of the southern struggle.[10]

This party will not emanate from the unions. There is no broad union movement in the South; only a few unions exist, owing their generally tenuous hold to special circumstances like a monopoly of skilled labor and contracts derived from national negotiations. These unions for the most part are lily-white, and insofar as they represent an aristocracy of labor, tend to be supporters of segregation. Nevertheless, they have no legal protection or legal avenues of expansion.

However, there are workers in the South and there are masses in motion who need an independent political party of their own; they are entitled to form a party called "Labor" or otherwise, with or without the participation of the unions.

Significant unionism will never exist in the South short of a new regime, for democratic rights are the foundation of unionism. Consequently, the causal relation between unionism and the labor party that characterizes the North is reversed in the South: *Southern unionism will not be the basis but the product of the labor party.*

## The strategic power of northern labor

The U.S. government will be even more hostile to the unfolding southern revolution than toward Cuba. It will see in the revolt the beginning of the socialist revolution in the United States—which, in fact, it will be.

The problem, therefore, arises of how to neutralize and/or paralyze the government's counterrevolutionary tactics.

Northern labor has such power. Thus, its support is decisive for the southern movement. But such support is precluded as long as unions remain impotent under bureaucratic rule.

A key task of northern Blacks is accordingly posed: activizing Black and white unionists into fighting for union democracy and a new leftwing leadership that will place the financial, organizational and political resources of labor at the disposal of the civil rights movement.

What a historical reversal—and triumph—this will be! The failure of the CIO's "Operation Dixie" fifteen years ago[11] was one of the important causes of worker demoralization that aided the bureaucracy in cementing its stranglehold on the unions. Along with the Taft-Hartley Act,[12] Operation Dixie signified the end of the union movement's ability to expand. It ushered in the era of cannibal unionism—expansion over the corpses of weaker or "Communist" unions—and crystallized the trend to flagrant class collaboration, sufferance of government domination, and arrogant white supremacy.

Labor's failure in the South, never adequately explained, disheartened many union militants; their confidence in their class was weakened. But the politicalization of the southern civil rights movement will spell out the racist cause of this defeat and give militants a new understanding, a fresh perspective, and a new opportunity to build unionism in Dixie.

A new hope for southern unionism will be raised in the northern labor movement when the civil rights movement starts requesting support for southern political action. The ferment in the working class will accelerate. Significant layers of northern workers will come to understand that their own democratic rights are vitally endangered by southern practice and its threatened northward extension.

Workers will want to strike a decisive blow in their own behalf by helping the cause of southern unionism, which demands in turn support to the democratic rights movement there.

Even sections of the labor bureaucracy fear the southern system. The runaway-shop South is the fountainhead of reactionary antilabor legislation and fascistic movements. Unionism's failure in the South is the Achilles heel of the bureaucracy, rendering it helpless before organizational erosion.

Northern labor officialdom today would have to listen to representatives of the impressive southern movement.

•　•　•

A dialectical interdependence links the southern labor party, southern unionism, and the left wing in northern unions.

In a police state, simple mass action (picket line, mass meeting, boycott, etc.) is not enough to win any democratic rights, including union recognition. Local tactics must be geared to the real nature of the oppressor, to interracial workingclass solidarity, and to active assistance by the northern Black and labor movements. This is the historical difference between union organizing in the 1930s and union organizing in the 1960s; the former demanded class struggle in a bourgeois democratic environment, but today we need political struggle against the iron heel of a brutal totalitarian state apparatus—the southern wing of U.S. capitalism.

The very *backwardness* of Dixie grips the more advanced northern labor movement by the throat, choking and stifling it; to survive, the North must break this stranglehold. Defense of the southern movement is the opening wedge in this struggle for self-preservation.

# The North: Prolonged crisis of leadership and quest for a program

## The reformist leadership

Whereas the southern movement is characterized by mass activism and the beginnings of ideological probing, the northern sector is only just becoming, by reflex, a mass movement, despite its more advanced level of political consciousness.

The South is proceeding swiftly and classically from action to thought; the more complex North has been studying programs and parties for 30 years and its passivity syndrome is the outcome of this frustrating search.

Uncertainty, accommodation, cynicism, or blind rage are not programs for action; they cannot mobilize. Only a call and a tactic—strike! boycott! sit-in!—can do that. The main "call" up North by Black leaders before the Till Case[13] and Montgomery was the NAACP's deadening "take it to court" refrain.

Reformism's decrepitude, only just unveiled down South, has been an acknowledged fact up North so long that it's generally accepted as a joke, like bad bus service.

Workingclass Blacks in the North, living amidst poverty and injustice, are generally conscious of the need for fundamental social change and have been for decades. Their economic position and their rejection by white society have rendered them immune to the American myth of a progressive, stable and benevolent capitalism supplying plenty for all. In the truth of their lives they find the truth—about American society.

This radical awareness, while undirected toward a specific means of social change, has expressed itself in an overwhelming response to every opportunity to demonstrate in breadth against the status quo: through the old Communist Party, the CIO, the March on Washington Movement,[14] wartime struggles, the SWP, racial wars in Harlem and De-troit, the Progressive Party, the Harlem reception of Fidel Castro, the pro-Lumumba[15] demonstrations, etc.

Consciousness has kept pace with reality. But in the ab-sence of a leadership adequate to the task, decades of dis-appointment and disgust ensued. Where mature objective conditions and mass consciousness exist without a leader-ship prepared to advance the struggle to higher levels, all elements of a crisis of leadership are present. The entire movement, denied the logic of its own dynamic, tends to degenerate.

What is the source of this protracted crisis of leadership?

The struggle against racial discrimination has centered around the demand for integration. The official leaders of the integration movement have come from the middleclass professionals. The inability of this leadership to express the needs of the masses and to develop an effective strategy is lodged in the contradictory position of the middle class in general, compounded by the peculiarities imposed by the race system.

The *ghetto petty-bourgeoisie*—the self-employed and the professionals—feed on the masses and often despise and fear them; at the same time, they are brutally rejected by white society and identified with their "inferiors."

On the one hand, they enjoy a racial monopoly of cer-tain businesses and occupations, thereby profiting from segregation; on the other hand, the flagrant gap between their living standard, and their social status outside the ghetto, is a source of daily humiliation and resentment against racism.

A conflict therefore exists between their class and racial interests. By turns cynical, conciliatory or enraged, they still exert a basically conservative pressure upon integration leaders, intensifying their hostility toward fundamental change and their habit of compromise and tokenism.

A less conservative but still restrictive pressure on the leadership stems from a section of the new middle class of *professionals and semiprofessionals* who are the main beneficiaries of integration struggles.

With good jobs in the white world (government, education, public institutions, and the white-collar sector of industry), this group sees individual assimilation as the goal. Theirs is "the desire to achieve acceptance in American life by conforming to the ideals, values, and patterns of behavior of white Americans" (E. Franklin Frazier[16]).

But the desire rarely can be realized. Revolving in a restricted circle of Black professionals and white liberals, they, too, are ambivalent. In limbo between two worlds, and unsure of their identity, they have no mass influence.

The leadership of the integration movement comes mainly from these two sectors and reflects their political schizophrenia. Pushed hard today by the ranks and national pressures into tough talk and occasional frenetic activism, they still more or less zealously guard their pro-capitalist respectability and conformism.

The failure of this middleclass leadership to inspire and advance the movement is caused by reformism. The old-style leaders can provide no solution to the elementary demands of the southern struggle, and they lock up the northern movement in capitalist politics.

There is no class/race conflict in the Black worker. The struggles for civil rights and workingclass solidarity are complementary and equal parts of the drive of the entire working class for emancipation.

Worker-leaders, however, have been rendered cautious by events. Unions, paralyzed by bureaucracy and government, remain essentially unmoved by civil rights struggles, whether inside or outside the unions. Black workingclass leaders within the unions become conservatized and intimidated by the class collaborationist passivity of the unions and by the shakiness of their own privileged jobs and higher incomes (relative to the community norm). At the present moment they provide no alternative leadership to that of the middle class.

From the early 1930s to 1950, advanced Black militants, numbering many thousands, dedicated themselves to leading the Black movement toward socialism, first through the Communist Party and, after 1941, through the SWP. But neither party was able to demonstrate convincingly its capacity to apply Marxism to the Black struggle.

This failure of theory and practice forced Blacks to seek solutions elsewhere or caged them in doctrinaire formulas. No substantial Marxist leadership was built, and the desire of socialist Blacks to lead the Black movement in a militant anticapitalist direction was blunted.

## The nationalist alternative to reformism

The contradictory and demoralizing coexistence of a reformist leadership with militant ranks has caused a certain revulsion-reflex against the principle of integration. Blacks are increasingly attracted to newly revived doctrines of separatism. But here, too, they are finding a leadership that is basically reformist and arbitrary, oriented elsewhere than the field of struggle.

Is there no alternative to the choice between reformist-conformist integration or a Black homeland? This 30-year-old dilemma can only be answered by Marxist analysis. What do logic, history and sociology provide in the analysis of the Integration — Nationalism — Separatism complex?

*A nation, according to orthodox Leninist definition, is a people united by an exclusive geography and a common heritage, language, history and mode of production, all comprising a distinctive culture.*

Nationalism had long been attained by the powerful nations of Western Europe when the developing Russian

Revolution revealed a new aspect of the National Question. Over a hundred small, oppressed nations and pre-national tribal peoples discovered or rediscovered national aspirations long throttled by Great Russian chauvinism but newly liberated by the economic crisis and the Bolshevik slogan of self-determination. These deep-seated national aspirations became a huge revolutionary centrifugal force, aiding in the destruction of the Czarist empire and the capitalist regime which followed, and making it possible for the Russian proletariat to win and hold the power.

Long before the revolution, Lenin oriented the Bolsheviks toward these backward, semi-feudal, agrarian peoples through his analysis of the National Question and the slogan of self-determination. This analysis became a new body of Marxist theory, guiding socialists in the task of awakening latent nationalist drives in order to strengthen the struggle against capitalism.

United States Blacks obviously do not fit into the classical definition of a nation. But it is contended that they nevertheless are a potential nation; that they may *become* a nation if and when they achieve a national consciousness. And what constitutes a national consciousness? According to the Socialist Workers Party, it is "a certain group of people, living in a certain place, [that] has decided to take its political destinies into its own hands."[17]

So at that point where Blacks fight in their own way for their own goals and with their own leaders, they apparently become transformed. They metamorphose from a race into a nation, the Black Question turns into the National Question, and the fate of Blacks suddenly becomes determined not by their own history in America, but by laws of national development deduced from the plight of small backward nations who collectively constituted the majority of the population of the Czarist empire.

This abstruse logic has nothing to do with Marxism, but sim-

*Writer Claude McKay represented revolutionary African Americans at the Fourth Congress of the Communist International in Moscow. The 1922 Congress passed a resolution of support for the worldwide struggles of Black people. (Clara Zetkin, international communist leader and feminist, far right.)*

ply revives the abstract-psychological definition of nationalism in preference to a concrete, historical materialist treatment.

In his sole contribution to Marxist thought, *Marxism and the National Question,* Stalin wrote: "A nation is a historically evolved, stable community of language, territory, economic life, and psychological makeup manifested in a community of culture."[18] Commenting favorably on this analysis, Trotsky wrote: "This combined definition, compounding the psychological attributes of a nation with the geographic and economic conditions of its development, is not only correct theoretically, but also practically fruitful, for then the solution to the problem of each nation's fate must perforce be sought along the lines of changing the material condition of its existence, beginning with territory."[19]

That Blacks are a potential "nation" is an unproved assumption. That Blacks constitute a "nation" or an "incipient nation" or an "emerging nation" or even a "nation within a nation" requires *concrete analysis,* rarely supplied.

For instance:

• If Blacks are not a classic nation, what *particular* aspects of nationalism in their condition make for the possible emergence of a national consciousness? ("Oppression" is no answer.)

• Granting, for argument's sake, that some concrete nationalist factors do apply, producing similarities, why is the right of self-determination the correct slogan? Might it just as logically *not* be correct given the differences? What is decisive here?

• How can a classic, nationally oppressed group directing its own destiny be equated to an oppressed group that is not a nation but is fighting for freedom? May a national consciousness be achieved by child-laborers, women,[20] atheists, migratory workers, aged pensioners, and sharecroppers?

• The Bolsheviks directed European nationalism into serving the revolution. Precisely how and why is Black separatism progressive and anticapitalist?

• Why does the relatively advanced and exploding Black struggle need the type of slogan designed to raise the consciousness of a very backward, agrarian European or Eurasian tribal people?

• If a dormant nationalism will awaken under conditions of self-awareness and crisis, how do we explain the rejection of separatism by Blacks over a 300-year period of revolutions, revolts, wars, upheavals, etc.?

Answers to questions like the above are almost invariably based on abstractions from international experience, not on the powerful realities and extraordinary history of the Black people in the United States. Marxists tend to minimize the voluminous works of Black scholars who investigated and dissected the Black Question, but their opinions are weighty and must be respected.

## Racial segregation: A unique oppression

Great Black scholars such as O.C. Cox, E. Franklin Frazier, James W. Johnson, and Alain Locke consistently maintain that the Black Question is a unique race question, that the kind of oppression suffered by Blacks in the United States is unique in history, and that never before on earth has a group been persecuted purely because of skin color, i.e., race.

What is race? It is not a valid biological category. It is a *social relation*. It arose out of capitalist necessity to justify the slave trade and human chattel slavery to a western world which was simultaneously discovering the inalienable "rights of man" and social justice. Thus the fictions of race superiority-inferiority and the nonhuman nature of Blacks were invented.

In the southern United States, with its unlimited expanse of virgin land, slavery took firm root.

Initiated by mercantile capitalists, the southern slave system became more powerful than its founders, producing an independent ruling class which eventually governed the entire United States.

The pervasive economic and political power of the slave owners disfigured American society from the outset by imposing upon the entire nation the ideology of white supremacy, the hypocrisy and irrationality of race and race relations, and tolerance of the horrors of chattel slavery.

After the Civil War and Reconstruction destroyed the old slave-owning class, northern capital, from economic and political motives, betrayed its promises and created a revised, capitalist form of race relations based upon many of the traditions and social relations of slavery. *Segregation* took the place of the chattel slave as the main prop of the new racist order.

An analysis of this tortuous history reveals that race, i.e., race relations, is a peculiar and independent category of social relations. As compared to historically necessary social categories—class, nationality, caste—race is *irrational*.

Social relations deriving from class, nation, etc., may be unjust, oppressive, and reactionary, yet these categories have a material foundation in modes of production and play progressive roles during certain historical periods. The class struggle itself is nothing less than "the motive force of history."

Race exploitation, on the other hand, has no necessary relation to any mode of production. A system of exploitation and discrimination revolving around the axis of skin color, it is arbitrary and perverted, and serves no progressive function whatsoever. It has caused American society to become organized around race relations, and, therefore, around prejudice.

The race consciousness of white workers supersedes even their class consciousness, dulling their minds, doubling the obstacles for Blacks, and preventing the organization of the proletariat as a class.

Because of the utter irrationality of race as a reason for social partition, segregation is absolutely required for the perpetuation of racial exploitation, and because of this interdependence of segregation and discrimination, the Black movement for nearly two centuries has directed its main line of struggle against segregation—against that barrier which prevents Americans from becoming a whole people, from becoming themselves.

### The race question and the National Question

Can't we, nevertheless, call the Black Question a National Question because of some similarities?

Not without denying its unique character. The Black Question is not merely different from the National Question, it is diametrically opposed to it.

• Segregation is no factor whatsoever of national oppression. On the contrary, forced assimilation is the rule and mode of oppression.

• In oppressed nations, the bourgeoisie tends toward assimilation with the oppressor; among Blacks, the bourgeoisie (the small but rich capitalist class) is the only consistently pro-segregation class.

• Separatist movements among oppressed nations are almost universally progressive and liberating in philosophy and ideology, concretely attacking the institutions and practices of the national oppressor. But Black separatist movements have all accommodated to the form of oppression—segregation. They accept and cater to the irrational category of race underlying social division into Black and white. Some Black separatist movements have been militant, but only within the framework of retrogressive concepts. Other separatist movements objectively capitulated to white supremacy on almost every score.

• The historic drive of oppressed nations is towards separatism; the historic drive of U.S. Blacks is against separatism and segregation.

• For an oppressed nation to become integrated is a reactionary concession to the status quo, a defeat; integration for Blacks is revolutionary, because American capitalism incorporates segregation in its fundamental structure and cannot survive without it.

• Potential and pre-nations, once aroused, have no difficulty in perceiving a qualitative difference of identity in themselves and their oppressor. Blacks are Americans in nationality according to all basic criteria, and they recognize the unfair, white-imposed color line as the central difference between them and whites.

Among the oldest nonnative inhabitants of this country, the Black people have contributed a huge share to U.S. wealth, progress and world preeminence.

Blacks have played heroic and sometime decisive roles

in all the historically important developments of the country. Their lives are inextricably involved with whites. Precisely because this is their homeland, prejudice and discrimination are infuriating. There is no other home; Afro-Americanism doesn't indicate a previous nationality, for a continent is not a nation, and U.S. Black culture and customs do not derive from any particular African nation. Indeed, Blacks rarely know where in Africa their ancestors lived, and they often feel strange with Africans (and vice-versa). The affinity for Africa is racial and internationalist.

Africans themselves are Pan-Africans first and nationals second. In defiance of the laws of European national development, the African revolution pushed *national sovereignty* into the background of its independence struggles almost from the beginning.

In Kenya, for example, the Kikuyu gave their military-defensive organizations not national but continental designations, such as "The African Fighting Forces" and "Defense Council of the Whole of Africa, Kenya Branch."

*Africa for the Africans* is the central rallying slogan of the revolutions on that continent. The strictly national aspirations of the peoples of Black Africa (scores of nations and incipient nations, most of which had few or no relations with each other historically) have long been superceded by *race consciousness,* deriving from the added burden of racial oppression under colonialism.

What is commonly called African "Nationalism" is more accurately described as African Internationalism.

• • •

On every score, the Black Question stands by itself as a unique phenomenon among exploited minorities, demanding independent analysis based on the key factors of *race and segregation.* To lump it together with its opposite, with

European nationalism, obscures its character and its goals.

Do the transitory forms of the Black struggle for existence reveal or conceal its real nature? When the movement does assume nationalist-like forms, are these expressions representative or singular?

Again, logic and history must provide the clues.

## Black separatism

Black "Nationalism," an expression of race consciousness, assumes the extreme form, *under certain conditions,* of separatism. An examination of the main historical expressions of separatism will illustrate the nature of these conditions and the ensuing character of the organizations.

### The American Colonization Society

The first "Back to Africa" movement was initiated by the slave owners in 1800—the American Colonization Society.

The plantation system had become transformed from a dying tobacco economy into a flourishing cotton economy, and the new wealth of the southern oligarchy took political form in the tremendous power it wielded over the U.S. government. The plantation aristocracy was determined to expand the slave system and eliminate antislavery agitation, but free Black abolitionists posed a serious threat to them.

The slave owners instigated a wave of terrorism against the slaves, and, through their domination of the White House and Congress, unleashed similar intimidation against northern freed Blacks.

The trend toward emancipation begun by the first American Revolution was reversed. This turn of events caused white society to desert and completely isolate the free Blacks. But the slave owners had a solution for them—subsidized deportation. And this program proved popular with a large section of freed slaves who couldn't survive in the prevalent economic and political climate of reaction.

In a reflex born of desperation, free Blacks joined the colonization movement, and thousands went to Liberia.

The separatist recoil ended abruptly in 1817 after the emergence of the first national organization of free Blacks, the *Convention Movement.* Its first meeting repudiated the Colonization Society and laid down the principle of "stay where you are and fight for immediate and unconditional emancipation."

This decisive turning point in the Black struggle laid the foundation for abolitionism.

## The Garvey movement

The Garvey "Back to Africa" campaign emerged from three key sources: the accommodationist doctrine of Booker T. Washington, the exclusivist "Talented Tenth" nature of the NAACP,[21] and the growth of Harlem and industrial employment for Blacks during World War I.

Booker T. Washington reflected the dismal hopelessness of Blacks after the agonizing and bloody defeat of Reconstruction. Adapting to reaction, he proclaimed acceptance of segregation, creating a doctrine for Blacks that echoed the judicial formula of "separate but equal" (1893). In the absence of any channel for mass struggle, he accepted Black inferiority as a premise and the race-structure of the South as a virtue. He urged industrial education to "fit" Blacks and called integration "folly."

These concepts were quickly negated by William Monroe Trotter and W.E.B. DuBois, who eloquently rejected the doctrine of separatism and exposed its source in the oppressor. DuBois organized Black intellectuals for leadership of the movement; they shook up the white liberals with their revelations of the horror of the New South and built a legal and propaganda apparatus for the movement—the NAACP (1909).

World War I labor shortages caused southern Blacks to migrate to the North, where industrial employment considerably increased their income. Harlem became the center of the Black world. The Black movement, no longer an agrarian body of ex-slaves terrorized by the KKK, began to recover its social energy.

But the NAACP was oriented elsewhere, and Marcus Garvey, a West Indian unscarred by defeat and uninhibited by sophistication, stepped into the breach.

Starting with Booker T. Washington's doctrine of separate but equal, he added the old "Back to Africa" slogan and the new "Buy Black, Live Black, Think Black" idea, injecting hope and defiance into Washington's doctrine of despair and turning it on its head.

In 1916, he began the Universal Negro Improvement Association in Harlem, launching a meteoric career. For the "Redemption of Africa" he created, in Harlem, an entire "government," including an "aristocracy" (Duke of the Nile, Overlord of Uganda, High Potentate of Africa, etc.) dazzling uniforms, the Black Legion military guard and elaborate rituals. He presided as "Provisional President of the Empire of Africa."

A century before, the "Back to Africa" movement had meant exactly what it said: it repatriated thousands of free Blacks to Liberia. But very few Blacks in the Universal Negro Improvement Association wanted to go back. They chanted "Back to Africa" as a means of protesting their intolerable condition in white America. They demanded dignity and economic security in the United States.

Garvey understood this. Accompanying "Back to Africa" was the slogan "Black Star Line"—a projected Black-owned-and-operated steamship company which served the dual purpose of symbolizing the Return to Africa and providing a program for a Black economy in the United States.

"Rise up you mighty giant!" Garvey exhorted. "Trade

among yourselves and trade with Negroes abroad. Build a Negro Church based upon African religion, Negro schools, and a Negro society."

The UNIA was the most powerful Black movement of its era, representing a genuine social awakening of the Black masses after defeat, yet it neither confirmed the correctness of Washington's philosophy nor the separatist nature of the Black movement. It was a vehicle of protest upon the only ground open to Blacks in that time of continued isolation: internal community self-organization and activity.

It proved that race uplift, black business and a militant spirit were not enough to hold a movement together indefinitely or serve as a vehicle of direct struggle against oppression.

The predominance of Garveyism in the Black community proved transitory. Rent by internal contradictions and crises, it evaporated as soon as realistic instead of romantic avenues of resistance to racial discrimination opened.

This occurred in 1925 when the organization of the Brotherhood of Sleeping Car Porters was achieved, merging Black socialist leadership with the proletarian struggle. In alliance with the NAACP, these new workingclass leaders undertook a campaign for jobs in Harlem, popularizing labor unionism and paving the way for later Black entrance into the main stream of workingclass struggle—the CIO.

There have been minor separatist movements, such as that in the early 1930s for a *49th State*. This was an attempt by the Black bourgeoisie to turn the movement away from integration opportunities offered by interracial trade unionism. It never received popular support, nor have other separatist groupings until recently.

The only two separatist movements since 1800 which attracted mass support—Colonization and Garveyism—were

*Marcus Garvey (1887-1940) and Elijah Muhammad (1897-1975) led Black separatist movements that emerged at times when other avenues of mass struggle had been closed.*

*transitional* vehicles to higher stages of struggle which repudiated separatism. They both served a function in the Black movement, but never represented an important historical objective of Blacks. Rather, they were a mode of existence after demoralization and/or the closing of mass avenues of struggle. In both cases when doors of struggle opened, separatism, always born of demoralization, disappeared.

### The Black Muslims

The Black Muslims are the latest major separatist movement, resulting somewhat from the isolation of the Blacks from the labor movement, but more specifically from the closing of the doors of struggle by the bankrupt northern reformist leaders.

The Muslims' anti-conformist and anti-reformist posture strikes a responsive chord among the most exploited sections of the unrepresented Black workers. The Muslims' ruthless unmasking of race reality in the United States through blistering attacks on the ideology and practice of white supremacy and the discredited Black gradualists and opportunists reflects and deepens the wisdom of their audiences.

Through their businesses and schools, the Muslims train men for jobs and women for domestic virtue; they rehabilitate former habitués of police court and prison, and offset degeneration among the demoralized and backward. They project, like Garvey, an economic program for Black business, both cooperative and private, within the ghetto, heightening race consciousness and community solidarity through this program. Such proposals do bring needed money into the Black community through jobs and surplus value.

But like all previous separatists, the Muslims are ambiguous; they embody retrogressive as well as progressive ideas, utopian as well as rational objectives.

Their organization is militaristic and autocratic. Their schools preach a doctrine of defensive racism, absolute male supremacy, anti-Semitism, descent from Allah, and cosmic vengeance. Their call for an independent state opens no channel for struggle against oppression. Their concept of Black business as a cure-all is utopianism in classic form.

Many analysts have noted the "pathetic" aspect of the Muslims—their wild reach for a glamorous identity. This is a byproduct of the post-World War II trend among some Black intellectuals to disdain the study of Black history and culture, equating it with the segregationists' glorification of Uncle Tom. Black leaders, subsequently, not only had no program but no historical race identity and race tradition to offer. The Muslims had both. An old program— but a new God and a new invented identity, which imparted to some of the poorest Blacks a new sense of security and solidarity.

So once again, in the absence of a realistic and inspiring program of action, mysticism, razzle-dazzle and speak-

bitterness became the mode of existence for sections of the most oppressed.

Much more serious, however, is the Muslims' sectarian abstention from struggle, as graphically revealed in Birmingham. Amid the greatest mass actions in the modern South, they scoffed from the sidelines. After the demonstrations subsided and the results were in, they did a brisk business in memberships on the following basis: they wrote off the tremendous mass experience, from which such rich lessons are being learned, as a dismal defeat proving the folly of struggle!

### Garvey and the Muslims—a comparison

Incapable of fundamentally advancing the struggle, the Black Muslims actually retard it in their own way, no less than the Wilkinses and the Kings. While similar to the Garvey movement in every respect, they suffer considerably by comparison.

*Approach to history*

Garvey introduced Black American workers to their real heritage in Africa. He popularized the findings of the integrationist scholars, building race pride in the truly dramatic historical achievements of Black Africa.

The Muslims, connecting Blacks to Islam, have produced an absurd fiction. Moslem Arabs were the original organizers of the African slave trade and partners with the Christians in devastating the pagan tribes and nations of central and western Africa.

*Internationalism*

Garvey's "Africa for the Africans" protested white imperialist domination of Africa, inspiring race solidarity and internationalism among American Blacks and vitally stimulating Africans. Garvey accomplished perhaps as much as the great W.E.B. DuBois in awakening the Pan-African revolution from afar. Independently, these implacable foes, each possessed of long-range historical vision, helped to create that interpenetration of the African and U.S. Black struggles that had such revolutionary consequences in Africa and pose such revolutionary implications for the United States.

The Muslims offer Africa nothing. They even deprive it of its rightful place in the heritage and politics of U.S. Blacks.

### Religion

After the defeat of Reconstruction, the Black movement ebbed back into religion, which provided virtually the only expression of the mass aspiration for a better life. While the Garvey movement was by no means devoid of mysticism, it represented the first mass development away from post-Reconstruction religious expression of discontent. The UNIA was a *social protest organization* wherein religion took a distinctly subordinate place.

The Muslims are a religious organization, luring essentially rationalistic proletarians backward into the Temple. The Temple is the focal point; the condition for participation is religious conversion.

### Politics

In the political field, the Muslims are more astute than the Garveyites, who served the Booker T. Washington Republican Party machine. Should the Muslims activate their threatened plunge into politics and maintain the contempt they now affirm for the existing white political structure, they would find themselves involved in a profound anti-capitalist struggle whose logic would force them to seek political rather than racial allies. A crisis of their own ideology would result, severely shaking their organization.[22]

## The Black nationalism of white radicals

Until the complete Stalinization of the Comintern in the 1920s, the radical movement in the United States was vaguely integrationist.

The IWW (Industrial Workers of the World), militantly interracial, recognized no special Black Question; it was a class question, like everything else, to be solved through industrial unionism.

The Socialist Party and Communist Party attitudes are aptly reviewed by John Reed in his report to the Second Congress of the Comintern in 1920:

...The old SP undertook no serious attempt to organize. In several states the Negroes were not accepted into the Party; in others they were separated into special sections; and in the Party units in the South, in general, spending Party money on propaganda among Negroes was forbidden.

...[After World War I] *The Messenger* was founded, edited by a young Negro Socialist named Randolph. The magazine combined Socialist propaganda with a call to race consciousness...but at the same time... insisted on closest union with the white workers despite the fact that at times they took part in the pogroms on Negroes.

Among [Negroes] arose and exists a movement for an armed uprising against the whites. Negro soldiers, returning from the front, were organized for self-defense... Communists, strongly in favor of a Negro movement for self-defense, must at the same time speak out against the idea of a separate uprising of Negroes... [which] without the support of the white proletariat... would only be a signal for the counterrevolution.

> Every movement aimed at an independent national existence does not meet with success among Negroes, as, for example, the "Back-to-Africa" movement which existed several years ago. They consider themselves first of all Americans whose home is the U.S. This greatly simplifies the problem for Communists. The policy of the Communists towards Negroes should be to look at them first of all as workers.

> ...the Communists must not stand aside from the movement of the Negroes for social and political equality which now, at the moment of growth of race consciousness, has widely developed among the Negro masses... Social revolution...will be the only means of liberating the Negro as an oppressed nation.[23]

But Garvey's mass support in the 1920s was very impressive. Stalin sent a Comintern representative to the 1929 Jamaica convention of the Garvey movement to debate the question, "Should Negroes join the Comintern?" Garvey won.

That same year ushered in the "Third Period" of international Stalinism, characterized by an anti-reality adventuristic program which took form on the Black Question in the imperative slogan of "Self-Determination for the Black Belt." Not only was the now-obvious *independent and special* nature of struggle equated to nationalism, but separation was proclaimed as the only revolutionary course.

White Communists promptly undertook a search for some historical foundation to this theory. They sought to discover the national peculiarities of Blacks and they tried dutifully to uncover separatist trends which would verify their prognosis: that Blacks were an incipient nation needing only to have their consciousness and will to struggle awakened in order to discover that what they really wanted all along was a separate territory, independent government and racial exclusiveness.

The research yielded meager results. Its continuity was regularly disrupted by the twists of Kremlin policy which alternately injected self-determination during leftish periods and withdrew it during ultra-rightist swings. Communist militants thereafter came to identify self-determination with "real Leninism" and with Foster,[24] while integration was associated with "social-democratic reformism" and Earl Browder.[25]

The Trotskyist leadership (apparently with the exception of at least Oehler[26]) took the position that not a national but a racial question was involved and that the struggle for civil rights, not racial autonomy, was the militant anti-capitalist direction of motion.

From the meager documentary material available, it would appear that while they didn't have a fully worked-out position, they had basically correct political instincts on this question, and these were brought before Trotsky in Turkey in 1933.

Trotsky, suspicious of a political organization in a bi-racial country composed exclusively of the dominant race, defended the basic nationalist line of the CP (1933 Conversations).[27] He stated that while his knowledge of the U.S. Black Question was too inadequate for a decisive opinion, he discerned in the American attitude a similarity to Rosa Luxemburg[28] and to the reformist Social Democrats on the issue of the Eastern European nationalities.

The only thing he urgently proposed, however, was an immediate and thorough discussion of the question in the party (the Communist League of America), but apparently no such discussion was held. United States Trotskyism on the Black Question proceeded to grow over into its opposite: from integration to nationalism. This process was crystallized in the SWP's 1939 resolution, committing the party to nationalism and the right of self-determination.

So from 1929 on, as the modern integration movement gained steam, no radical parties could clearly understand the revolutionary implications of integration. The spectre of nationalism and its corollary principle of self-determination hovered constantly over the Black Question, with confusing results.

## Political inconsistency

White radicals could support integration only tentatively because they expected the Black movement to "mature" and reject integration. They tended to equate integration with the opportunism of petty-bourgeois intellectuals, and confidently awaited the "decision" for a separate nation, the only goal capable, they believed, of inspiring and activating the backward mass.

Where integration cannot be supported in theory or principle, it is very difficult to project a consistent strategic or tactical orientation towards it. At best, virtually all that can be done is to support from the outside and initiate small-scale action from the inside. This stance is politically uncomfortable.

## Political neutrality

White radicals, uncertain about the issue, agreed to "wait and see" and "hold the door open." This often inhibited their participation in the ideological discussion within the Black community. It is difficult to participate if one really does not know what the goal of Blacks is. Also, if Marxism-on-the-Black-Question means the right to choose separatism, neutral white radicals must make this offer to militant Blacks. The result sorely tries radicals' neutrality; their generosity and democratic spirit go unappreciated, at best. A Black radical fares little better.

As the astute French observer Daniel Guérin described:

> The formula runs the risk of offending them. By dangling before the Negroes the bait of "right of self-

determination," the white Stalinists expose themselves to the danger of seeming to want to impose upon them a new form of segregation, to relegate them to a new "ghetto." But it is not certain that the Negro masses, despite their "nationalism," deliberately want separate institutions. It seems more probable that they aspire to being treated, in all phases of their life, on an equal footing with whites.

In fact, the slogan of the "Negro nation" never stirred more than a very feeble echo in the Negro population. It was even badly received in the beginning by the Negro Stalinists, who finally had to yield, reluctantly, to the imperious orders of Moscow...

The only point on which the Stalinists saw correctly is this: the Negro masses have "nationalist" tendencies and will participate in the struggle to establish socialism in the U.S. only if this overall struggle is accompanied by a special struggle for the emancipation of the Negro race as such.[29]

It proves impossible in life to support the right of self-determination and also stay neutral on separatism.

Lenin frankly designed the slogan of self-determination to awaken the desire for a national state among backward agrarian people previously deprived of an opportunity to consider whether or not they wanted one. He wished to arouse this desire because of its highly likely revolutionary consequences for both the oppressed nation and the revolution as a whole. However, he said, having created and encouraged the desire for a national state, the party, to be tactful, might officially take a "hands off" position in order not to prejudice discussion of the problem. But, basically, it was understood that to issue the slogan was to extend an *invitation to separatism.*

To support the right to self-determination, then, is to invite separatism. The purpose of raising the slogan is not to show how democratic or impartial the party is, but to express precisely its *partiality* for a particular course in acceptable terms—as a choice which the nation has a right to make, rather than an injunction from the party. There can be no ambiguity on this score. By its very nature, the slogan is inferentially pro-separatist. Both Black and white workers understand it to be pro-separatist. And in a country where separatism connotes the old Separate but Equal, or a new form of self-segregation, this slogan is like a hot potato, making impossible a genuine neutrality on separatism.

Many white Marxists, particularly leaders of the SWP, rationalize their support of self-determination on the grounds that "the Black people haven't spoken yet."

It may be that the white people have not heard them yet. Not in thirty years, or one hundred years, or three hundred years of resistance, can any predominant direction of motion be cited by white "Nationalists." History, empirical evidence, the universality of the integration struggle—all lose meaning as the inevitable question mark is stamped upon every stage and facet of the movement. Since little can be proved or known in advance of the Year of Decision, the door must ostensibly always be left open to either variant. The intense commitment of Blacks to winning their demands, here and now, is adjudged inconclusive, as are the integrationist principles of the foremost Black analysts of the struggle.

Neutrality in operation becomes the practice of viewing the integrationist surge as indecisive or "peculiar" (in terms of theory) and welcoming any separatist signals as significant.

In granting to Blacks the right to decide to separate, many white radicals who claim neutrality seem to have appropriated the right to prejudge the decision.

## *Separatism and the freedom struggle*

Is there no place, then, for democratic self-determination? Don't Blacks have the right to decide their own fate?

Of course!—but in deference to their special history of oppression, not their "nationhood." A workers government in the United States could grant, as an elementary democratic right, an autonomous territory to Blacks, a section of Blacks or a tiny group of Blacks, should it be requested. But this has no earthly connection with the right of self-determination of small nations. This is a right which a workers government may offer to any special group having some cultural, religious, psychological, or other element in common which they want to preserve and which is not politically counterrevolutionary.[30]

The Soviet government granted the Jews a separate and autonomous national state in spite of the fact that the Bolshevik party had opposed Jewish separatism during the struggle against Czarism. Lenin had condemned the demand for the cultural autonomy of the ghetto as serving no purpose in the struggle. He never viewed the Jewish Question as a question of self-determination, precisely for the same reason that it does not apply to the U.S. Black Question: separatism provides no avenue of struggle against the fundamental institutions of oppression.

The essential question is not whether a workers state would grant national autonomy to a particular group on the basis of historically engendered cultural ties, but whether the struggle for separation is revolutionary and progressive under capitalism—whether it can indeed bring about freedom from economic, political and cultural oppression.

The unique feature of racial oppression is its *organization around segregation.* However determined may be the desires of some Blacks for a politically independent republic based on racial-cultural ties, the Black movement can grapple with oppression under capitalism only by attacking segregation. Separatism, by its very nature, cannot participate in this real struggle.

## The Black movement

Complex interrelations among Black history, segregation, the reformist leaders, the advancing mass consciousness, the backwardness of white labor and corruption of its leaders, radical theories, and the present international conjuncture have produced the current phenomenon called Black nationalism.

This movement is "nationalist" because, like the Africans, it wants an end to white domination and is prepared to wage war in its own behalf. But there the resemblance ends.

The chief components of the new upsurge—intolerance of gradualism and moderation and whites in general; independence, pride and responsibility; a now-or-never, do-or-die defiance—add up to a powerful method of self-mobilization for justice through integration. *The movement fights independently, but not for independence; it moves separately and almost alone, but not for separation; it demands the freedom of an equal partnership, not a divorce.*

It is Black and not nationalist. It insists on its historically proven right to belong. Black "nationalism" is not classic nationalism; indeed, it isn't nationalism at all. It is simply the current form and stage of the drive for integration, a stage completely consistent with the needs of the struggle.

James Baldwin's prognosis of integrated disaster, the fellowship of the flames,[31] if an equalitarian society does not emerge from the struggle, is the final summing-up of this inexorable choice: integration or mutual disintegration. There is no room for a "nationalist" alternative.

Separatism is usually brandished as a threat (except by Muslims), as a pretended alternative and means of retribution. It is not the real goal; northern Black "nationalism," the most advanced ideological sector of the movement, joined forces with southern Black direct action to lead the entire movement into the demand for Freedom Now, which almost everybody is for. But this is an abstraction. The double-barreled question on today's agenda is: Freedom How? and Freedom for What?

The Freedom Now movement is independent, but not homogenous.

In the South, forces are already assembling around the point-blank issue of Reform or Revolution. Northern political thinking, which has long grappled with the manifest crisis of leadership and absence of program, has evolved to an advanced point on the bridge to revolutionary internationalism. And this stage is symbolized by the "cultural" dilemma, the growing rejection of "white" values.

## The impact of Black culture on American society

Black slaves created a distinctive culture—a philosophy of life expressing the greatest aspirations for freedom of any people of the era; a thoroughly equalitarian and democratic attitude; a folk art in story and song; and a musical speech.

Distinguishing this culture from the national cultures of Europe was the fact that it was never circumscribed, isolated or exclusive. On the contrary, it rapidly inundated the transplanted Anglo-Saxon culture of the slave owners. In the rest of the country a cultural vacuum prevailed, born of the melting pot, of class fluidity, of constant migration and immigration. The vacuum acted like a sponge in absorbing Black folk culture. It was readily apparent that the chief barriers between Black and white were sociopolitical, not cultural, and that whites basically needed and responded to the Black culture.

White culture was predominantly European in areas

such as art, literature, classical music, theatre, the key religions, education, political principles, and Puritan morality. What was original to U.S. culture were certain progressive institutions—the plebeian folk-hero, democratic and informal manners, the relatively advanced position of women, unionism, the public school, individualism and free speech, and many more—reflecting America's unusual economic and political conditions. But these were all corrupted by the victory of Jim Crow and segregation following Reconstruction.

Denied the opportunity to further absorb Black creativity, white American culture was left in a feeble state. The mores and habits of the imperialist "robber barons" took over. This new capitalist class, produced by the Civil War, stamped its ruthless, vulgar and Philistine image on American thought. A new house of culture was built upon White Supremacy and American Superiority—"The United States of Lyncherdom" (Mark Twain). And not until jazz artists and Black workers came north and the Black cultural Renaissance exploded in Harlem, did 20th century America start anew to create unique forms such as the modern novel, theatre, music, dance, movies, mass industrial unions, and organized sports.

Still, the predominantly racist culture holds sway today in the "materialistic, TV crazy...H-bomb wielding paradise of the white man" (Robert Vernon), a mean culture that embodies little humanity or truth. Artificial, hypocritical and sanctimonious, this culture is easily exploited by the master class for its sinister ends.

The feeling of cultural and psychological alienation among Blacks is at bottom a political rejection of capitalist practices and standards, a political view shared by most of the people in the world and by many white Americans.

Blacks may reject everything "white," but their own humanistic culture, expressed by way of bitter honesty, cutting sarcasm, and insult, is hardly *non*white—and is enormously popular with whites, as witness the success of comedian Dick Gregory. An exclusive Black culture today is an impossibility, for it has no geographical base; though born in the ghetto, it swiftly escapes and becomes

*"Street Life—Harlem" (1939) by Black artist William H. Johnson. The Harlem Renaissance of the 1920s and '30s was an unprecedented flourishing of African American expression in literature, art, music, dance, and drama.*

everybody's. And while this phenomenon is resented by some people of both races, it is precisely Black cultural expression in music, literature, speech, dress, dance, sports, style, and theatre that originally attracts many whites to the Black cause and the human cause. White youth especially feel passionately involved; they have to help, and how long they "stay on the train" will be determined by the level and momentum of the struggle.

Earlier demands of the integration movement, as expressed by DuBois, for instance, took cognizance of Blacks' need to value and cherish their own culture and outlook, to learn their history, and to affirm the identity that chauvinism had all but destroyed.

But reformist integrationists were ashamed of their slave heritage and culture. Racial equality to them meant that Blacks should become just like whites. Many Blacks, appalled at what they were supposed to become just like, have reversed direction.

They feel the need to halt the tendency to aspire to social assimilation. They intend to reestablish their own special identity and viewpoint as the condition of any future assimilation. "Black is Good," they say, and while they demand the reconstruction of society on a nonracial basis, they are unwilling to vanish as Blacks from the American scene, dissolving into white America.

Cultural alienation for any American objectively signifies a rejection of imperialist standards and capitalist ethics. That Black self-differentiation from white Christian evil is growing signifies not a national peculiarity but an advanced class-consciousness, which, like everything else about the Black movement, is *contagious*. Black cultural dissociation is showing the way to the white workers, the "enemy," reminding them of their youthful past and encouraging their future resistance to the status quo and propensity for social struggle.

## A vanguard of the class struggle

Freedom for What, even expressed in cynicism, is a serious question that can only be answered by socialism. And in the coming merged interracial struggle for jobs for all, homes for all, schools for all, unions for all, free speech for all, and antiwar for all, the white worker-devils will have their historic chance for culture, i.e., for class solidarity and revolutionary politics.

Even now, when mass protest marches and meetings are called, whites are invited and respond. The most impressive recent mass actions of the northern movement, generated by solidarity with the southern movement but utilizing the occasion to protest local conditions, all included whites. When people are in motion, en masse, their momentum dwarfs their prejudices. In Seattle, the young ministers who originated the protest march after Birmingham, publicly demanded that the white clergy and politicians join them!

That Blacks should lead white workers in social awareness, militancy and class solidarity is an illustration of the vanguard role they play, and the next likely arena for its expression will be the trade union movement.

Black trade unionists must serve a triple-headed master: whites, the boss and the union officialdom. The hand of bureaucratic intimidation, corrupting and stifling the white unionist, presses even more heavily on the Black unionist. Black workers find themselves in a peculiarly contradictory position—on the lowest rungs in the shop but on a relatively privileged economic level inside the ghetto. The latter status restrains their resistance to the bureaucracy; the former status drives them to seek a means of advancement compatible with the climate and the special problem of skin color.

Behind this contradiction lies the history of U.S. unionism. The craft unions in the United States have always been almost exclusively white, some incorporating racial exclusion in their constitutions. The organization of industrial workers, however, was impossible without the Black workers, and racial equality within the unions and plants became a principle of the CIO in its militant formative years. This integration of the basic work force of the nation had a revolutionary effect on racial relations throughout the country, projecting the civil rights struggle into an issue of central importance in American politics and setting the stage for the current movement for Black liberation.

During the post-World War II years, however, the CIO increasingly began to resemble the business unionism of the AFL. The bureaucracy in the CIO, with the help of the Taft-Hartley Act and the anti-communist campaign, got rid of the more radical and class-conscious unionists and established a new base resting on the more privileged, more conservative, and, hence, more prejudiced workers. The red purge fell heaviest on the more integrated unions. The Marine Cooks and Stewards disappeared from the face of the earth, while the West Coast longshoremen, mine-mill workers, and the coal miners were driven out of "official" organized labor.

The fusion of the CIO and AFL, instead of stimulating the organization of workers, turned out to be a last-gasp attempt of the bureaucracy to unite itself politically for a fight within the Democratic Party.

This unity was only made possible by the degeneration of the CIO, and underlined the facts that the entire union movement was now united behind the government and had incorporated the national racial structure into its organizations. The lily-white, racist labor bureaucracy, chained to the Democratic Party was incapable of moving towards organization of the millions of nonunion workers.

The growing prevalence of the ideology and practice of racism in the unions is one of their characteristics in the epoch of imperialist decay, and is both a cause and gauge of their degeneration. In return for selling out many of the rights and conditions won in the 1930s, the labor bureau-

DIALECTICS OF BLACK LIBERATION

cracy was awarded the consolation of becoming the guard-
ians of white supremacy in industry.

The Taft-Hartley Act closed the door on union expansion
even through class collaboration and dependence on the
government, thus stopping the growth of unionism and au-
tomatically shutting off unionism for the majority of Blacks.

The red-baiting purges, which immediately followed,
placed the unions firmly in the hands of the largely white,
conservative aristocracy of labor, preventing further advancement of Blacks on the job or in the labor movement.

This lesson should be clear by now to those intimidated
Black reformist leaders who thought they could escape
some of the wrath of reaction by siding with it on the "Communist" issue. It was red-baiting which locked the door of
unionism on Blacks.

Black workers were left to their own fate outside the labor movement, a fate marked by skyrocketing unemployment, youth disorientation, and the shock of migrating
southern Blacks at discovering that their traditional trades were
the property of a white aristocracy in the North. They often
found themselves excluded even from the service trades, and
felt desperate. Automated out of cotton production, they were
deeply, if subconsciously, fearful that without a place in the
economy only genocide remained as their lot.

The Negro American Labor Council was formed in 1960
in an attempt to head off the accelerating ferment in the
ghetto over jobs, unions, seniority, upgrading, etc. But it
could not hold back the explosions: decertification suits,[32]
the Philadelphia picket line,[33] and the growth of independent Black caucuses—embryonic left wings in the unions.

These struggles, and the manner in which they are
conducted, are part and parcel of the high class-
consciousness and basic union loyalty in the Black community, no matter what the pitch of resentment and indignation over their treatment by the labor aristocracy. Just as

Blacks fought fiercely against right-to-work laws, and in some cities led the fight, in these latest eruptions they show white jobless and unskilled workers in Philadelphia how to proceed when most avenues are blocked.

The Black unionist occupies a most strategic position in U.S. life today—that intersection where the civil rights and union movements connect and merge. In their own way, Black unionists are transmitting the dynamic of the one sector to the passivity of the other. They are igniting the spark that will get the left wing of labor off the ground.

### Blacks and independent politics

A similar causal relation prevails in the sphere of independent class politics.

The reluctance of the Black movement to break from captivity in the Democratic Party in the North and West stems from the objective lack of an immediate realistic alternative that would effectively mirror its advanced political caliber. Blacks are a smaller minority in the North than they are in the South, and while they hold an electoral majority now in several metropolitan areas, they cannot by themselves be more than a political minority nationally. Their independent political spirit is deep-seated and of long duration, but their numbers, while growing, are few as compared to whites.

In terms of parliamentary politics, Black politicians realistically write off their areas of numerical strength in the South where Blacks do not vote and will not in the immediate future. The political stagnation of the labor movement encourages opportunistic deals by the Black reformist leaders, leaving no way out for the militants short of support to the few socialist candidates in the field. But the drive to independent political expression is strong, and as militant Black leaders embark on experimental attempts to end the bondage of their movement to the Democratic Party, they

*The Mississippi Freedom Democratic Party, spearheaded by radical grassroots leaders such as Fanny Lou Hamer (left) and Ella Baker (right), was a momentous political movement that threatened the hegemony of the Democrats but did not decisively break with them.*

come face to face with the alternatives of united front or people's front, labor party or people's party, independence or pressure-group politics.

Four years ago, Harlem Congressman Adam Clayton Powell[34] called for a "Third Force" in American politics. This represented a feeling among the more ambitious Black leaders that the tremendous bargaining power inherent in the Black vote had been sold altogether too cheaply in the past. He proposed that the third force be the Black clergy. These "spiritual leaders" of the community could, if united, effectively manipulate the Black vote so as to wring substantial concessions on issues such as civil rights and Black candidates from either party. Via threats, revenge, and bargaining, they would reward their friends and punish their enemies.

Such a rehash of the old Gompers-AFL[35] policy is inherent in the concept of a political party that would unify the Black community, hold a balance of power, and engage in "practical" politics. While running independent local candidates where victory is assured and contesting some House of Representatives seats, such a party still would inexorably be drawn into supporting one capitalist politician over another, and finally one bourgeois party over another, inasmuch as its function is not to smash the old political foundations and create an entirely new labor party type of parliamentary majority.

Such a *vote-Black* unity party, containing everybody (diplomat Ralph Bunche,[36] Roy Wilkins, Rev. Powell, Rev. King, Malcolm X, the militants and radicals, etc.) could never be programmatically independent, and would shortly, like an American Labor Party[37] maneuver, deliver the Black vote *en toto* to the Democrats. Such a party, based on the now respectable, minimum, and formless plank of Freedom Now, would be a people's front of the minority, occupied with balance-of-power politicking.

Socialist support for a Freedom Now unity party apparently derives from a convergence of white Black-nationalism and trade unionism. With an anticipation amounting to certainty, radical socialists foresee an organizational break between the unions and the capitalist parties that will create a situation infused with revolutionary potential. But to superimpose the need for a labor party upon the Black movement is to see more than reality indicates. The Black movement is not a congress of trade unions, nor is it a nation. If it were either, an independent all-Black political party would be logical and viable. Since it is neither, an all-inclusive unity party is unrealistic and undesirable.

A truly independent party, on the other hand, with an anti-capitalist program and outlook, would not be a vehicle of political unity. Exactly the opposite: it would illuminate, clarify and polarize the discordant elements within the movement, creating an explosive class differentiation.

William Worthy's proposal for such a party emphasized the anti-capitalist program: antiwar, anti-imperialist, pro-colonial revolution, pro-social change.[38] Essentially, his is a call for a radical vanguard party, broadly if not explicitly socialistic. It is, in effect, an audacious move to unify the radicalized militants, who, if organized, would certainly exert a mass influence. But in order to ultimately unify the Black masses around a socialist perspective, the militants would have to wage the Bolshevik fight against very big guns—the powerful apparatus of the Powells, Kings, and others.

The present *united front* of the Black community is capable of massive and potent actions. Actual construction of an independent "unity" party, necessarily reformist, would deepen the internal class contradictions of the movement and threaten this unity in action—and for no good purpose. But to launch a Black radical vanguard organization would constitute an historic step forward.

• A Black vanguard party would furnish (a) a principled program, a rostrum, and an apparatus for independent Black candidates; (b) a graduate school for militants, specializing in political theory, the strategy of the struggle, and electioneering; and (c) an object lesson for the labor, peace and "progressive" movements.

• A Black vanguard party would assemble a resolute and dynamic new leadership for the Black united front, marking the beginning of the end of the long-thwarted quest for program and the paralyzing crisis of leadership.

# The revolutionary Marxist party in the Black struggle

## The record

The Marxist party has several parallel tasks in the Black struggle: theoretical, political, propagandistic, organizational, and agitational.

SWPers generally dismiss the complexity of these tasks by assuring doubters or critics that "We were right in '39, in '48, in '57. We are right today. Everything is going to be all right if we work hard and implement our decisions."

Yet rarely has such a vast social problem caused such extended difficulties and debates for Marxists. The record of the SWP is erratic, marked by high successes and deep crises, particularly in the key area of party-Black cadre relations. Confusion and discord have often prevailed over that 25 year period of always being right.

The SWP's intransigent advocacy of civil rights during and after World War II won the party and its press the support of thousands of workingclass Blacks. Black militants joined the party by the hundreds, providing both an excellent cadre and an opportunity to become a mass party of American workers. But this singular accomplishment is now completely lost. The SWP has squandered its political capital and injured its relationship to Blacks to such an extent that the Black exodus from the SWP had a far more profound effect upon the SWP than the similar exodus of Blacks from the CP had upon that organization.

Why? What is to be done about it? Why can't Marxists candidly come to grips with this sustained problem? If the proof is in the pudding, should the SWP not look to its recipe? Are more reverses and deeper isolation indicated before the SWP evaluates its theories, politics, propaganda, and organizational practices in depth? Either that, or as has been suggested, it must remain a white party to win white workers, so let the party stop fretting and get on with its main, white, business.[39] Yet the very fact that such proposals are made seriously and meet with agreement dictates the opposite course.

## Theory

What is SWP theory? Comrade Dan Roberts, in a 1957 statement defending the Political Committee position on the Little Rock crisis, wrote as follows about tendencies in the party:

> There are actually three points of view in the party on what has brought the civil rights issue to crisis proportions in the U.S. The point of view embodied in the last convention resolution holds that, while the Negro struggle was well under way in its own right, its advances do not explain the Supreme Court decision and other legal victories scored in recent years by the Negro people... Rather, we believe that what has made the civil rights issue such a paramount domestic concern in the past years has been the black eye that the Jim Crow system gives U.S. imperialism abroad and especially in the colonial world.

> A second viewpoint is the one advanced by Lois Saunders...and by Arne Swabeck... They see the main impetus to a sharpening of the civil rights question in Northern Big Business finding the Southern race system an obstacle to free investment of their capital in the South.

> Finally, Kirk [Fraser] holds that the acuteness of the civil rights issue is an accurate measure of the strength and revolutionary drive of the Negro people themselves and is caused directly by it.

While the above is somewhat oversimplified, and Saunders objected to the interpretation of her position, it provides a starting point: what are the various tendencies in the party on the Black Question?

There are at least six more or less distinct areas of opinion, not all clearly defined, and some overlapping. Nevertheless, they reflect the majority of the attitudes in the civil rights movement and on the Left.

### Black nationalism for white radicals

This broad tendency, discussed previously, holds that (a) integration ultimately is reformist and social democratic, and the demand for a separate state is the only *revolutionary* demand; or (b) either road may validly be chosen when the decision is made; or even (c) the Black Question is a National Question, but integration will be chosen.

Ironically, hardly had the ink dried on its 1939 nationalist resolution when there occurred an influx of militant integrationist Blacks into the SWP. Under the combined pressure of these workers and the integrationist movement of the 1940s, comrades adhering to nationalism generally restrained their views, never advancing them publicly and rarely privately. Consequently, until 1948, scores of new comrades never dreamed that self-determination was the official party line and never even heard of it. Blacks sensed something strange and ambiguous, and assumed it was prejudice. Tortuously expressing itself in policy, tactics, and social relations over the years, this ambivalence played its part in the alienation of almost an entire generation of Black revolutionaries.

### The Black Question as an appendage of trade unionism

This is not so much a theory of the Black Question as an unbalanced emphasis on trade unionism, an over-identification of unions with the working class, and a myopia about nonunionistic facets of the class struggle.

Not a formal doctrine, it is a prejudice in favor of trade unionism, giving rise to the feeling that the Black struggle, though independent organizationally, is tactically dependent upon the labor movement for virtually every move or advance—something like the Russian proletariat-and-peasantry relation.

In this connection, Daniel Guérin, in *Negroes on the March,* may be pardoned for dissociating himself from SWP maritime policy. On the West Coast, the white Deck and Engine Departments were equated to the proletariat while the largely Black Stewards Department was considered dependent and destined to follow the decisive proletariat. This is an atypical example, but illustrates the extremes to which this ideology may lead.

When unions are dormant, however, and the Black movement is obviously in motion, Black dependence is promptly shifted from unions to the colonial revolution or some other more "decisive" category.

Another characteristic of this tendency is its assumption that the Black movement is similar enough to the labor movement for the general laws of trade union development to apply.

For example: From the early 1940s until quite recently, a fetishism existed that the NAACP was the ordained organization of Black struggle, and to work in the militant National Negro Congress or to organize anything outside the NAACP would approximate the dual unionism of the CP's ultra-left period.

Because of this arbitrary subordination of the Black movement to a trade union principle, the Black cadre was imprisoned in the NAACP for years, unable even to probe the possibilities of independent, militant, and workingclass Black organization. Many Black comrades finally contrived their escape from this policy and from the party as well.

All party unionists are not of this opinion, and non-trade unionists may hold it. There are no rules in this tendency about what other theories its adherents may subscribe to. Some believe in integration, others adhere to extreme nationalism, etc. Both nationalism and trade union primacy entail the danger of reinforcing the prejudices of white workers, since nationalism offers a probable and endorsable segregated socialism, while unionism ascribes a dependent and subordinate role to the Black struggle.

### Economic determinism

The idea that the needs of production for skilled labor and an integrated work force require the capitalist class to do something drastic about the South is spurious and mechanical. Industrialists realize full well the long-term economic benefits of cheap, segregated labor.

### The activists

These include most of the Blacks in the SWP. They feel detached or skeptical about the theoretical discussion; the party has been discussing for years and nothing has changed very much. They are anxious for the party to collectively devise a means of intervening more effectively than has been the case, and they expect party leadership to take the lead in achieving this.

They are generally dissatisfied with party grasp of and performance in the Black movement, considering it inadequate. While they play their role in the transmission-link operation, informing the party of developing moods and groupings, they feel that no reciprocal levers for effective intervention are given them in exchange.

Outside the party they must cope daily with the hostile white world; inside the party, many resent having to criticize, complain or push, believing that awareness of the need for a better orientation and climate should be the entire party's responsibility and concern.

Some Black SWPers deduce that no meaningful interrelation of party and Black movement is currently objectively possible, and more fuel is added to the flame of separatism.

### The official compromise resolution

Here, the differences among all tendencies are usually softened and then "unified." The party is offered some integration, a great deal of nationalism, just enough separatism, much trade unionism, plenty of self-determination, a pledge of increased activism, a great deal of theoretical neutralism, and an overall injunction to wait and see.

Inasmuch as this type of resolution, speech, and article determines and expresses party theory over the years, it may be said that in terms of a guide to action, the party has no fundamental theory at all.

### Revolutionary Integration

That is the viewpoint expressed in this resolution. The Black Question is a unique racial, not national, question, embodied in a movement marked by integration, not self-determination, as its logical and historical motive force and goal. The demand for integration produces a struggle that is necessarily transitional to socialism and creates a revolutionary Black vanguard for the entire working class.

## Politics and propaganda

What does the SWP stand for?

It is difficult to know from week to week; it depends on what is read (bulletins, resolutions, *International Socialist Review, The Militant)* and which issue.

The 1957 convention resolution found the SWP rapt with admiration of the Reverend Dr. Martin Luther King.

Now, the Rev. Dr. King hasn't changed much, except that mass pressure keeps him very, very rushed. But King's obstructive reformism has been exposed by events, so the party has switched its allegiance to Elijah Muhammad, who, as head of the Black Muslims, is considered by the party to be today's most promising leader.

The SWP never acknowledges the crisis of leadership in the Black movement. The concept of "self-determina-

*Illustration from a 1945 SWP pamphlet on fighting segregation. Though the SWP wavered and erred in its analysis of the race question, it championed Black civil rights in the 1940s.*

tion," a revolutionary demand when used by the Bolsheviks, is denuded of all meaning and becomes a rationale for the SWP position that anyone who is leading at the moment is a good leader and a destined leader, regardless of program. Since Blacks are a "nation," they are politically homogenous and united; an anatomy of the class divergence among them is accordingly academic, because it is not decisive for a national movement. The important thing is to cement unity and not provoke dissension.

This attitude, of course, has nothing in common with a classic Trotskyist or Leninist approach to nationalism, but it prevails nevertheless.

Such vast tolerance for palpable opportunists on the part of the precise and authoritarian SWP leadership is nothing less than indulgence and paternalism.

Does the SWP have any criticism, constructive or otherwise, of the new leaders, tendencies, or organizations? Not publicly. Comrade Breitman made a timely and cogent criticism of CORE[40] and the Freedom Rides[41] in an internal bulletin. But there is almost never a word of such matters in the public press, although the rest of the Black and radical press does discuss such important and controversial issues. Articles criticizing the pacifist leadership of 1957 were refused publication in *The Militant* at that time, and such articles about the Muslims would meet a similar fate today.

The party has nothing to say about those ideas of the Black Muslims that are politically and socially obnoxious. On the contrary, it is considered slanderous to discuss them in this vein.

Similarly, disagreements from the field on *Militant* articles are referred to internal publication, and articles for *The Militant* containing a critical treatment of Black leaders are printed as letters. All this is properly within the province of responsible editing, but does not belong in the province of good politics. The editing merely serves SWP policy of nonintervention into political disputes unresolved as yet by all Blacks.

Having raised tail-endism to a political principle, the SWP does not even have any praise for new leaders and organizations which evolve out of the living struggle of the movement with a deepened political and revolutionary consciousness. James Baldwin, for instance, has been pushed out of a purely literary career into the civil rights struggle, where he carries tremendous weight with both whites and Blacks. He is conducting a running duel with separatism from a high level of racial sensitivity and a growing political awareness. He wrote of Mr. Muhammad, whom he loves and understands, "We would always be strangers, and possibly, one day, enemies."

James Baldwin has spoken, but the party is incapable of commenting (except for detached book reviews).

On every other kind of question, from community clubs to the international conjuncture, the party conceives its most elementary duty to be a clear statement of its position, particularly in regard to controversies. Class analysis is the Trotskyist tradition and strong point, and the SWP has solutions to political problems in China and Outer Mongolia.

But on the central question of the American revolution, the Black struggle, it can only report—and that very selectively. The party has no obvious political line except as reporters, and sometimes supporters, of what somebody else says. It does intervene politically when the trade unions are involved, as in the decertification suits, but since the interrelationship between the civil rights struggle and the union struggle is still a mystery to the SWP, it is usually wrong.

This one-sided neutrality becomes increasingly awkward as the party and press apprehensively keep hands off proliferating public disputes. How does this help Black comrades "to help the race form its opinion on separatism?" How does this help white comrades become better acquainted with the ideological pace of the Black struggle? The only thing the party and press have to tell members and supporters is that the Black movement, like the SWP, is always generally right and doing well.

Theoretical and political confusion run rampant as the SWP pragmatically changes its line with every new conjuncture. For years, over our strong opposition, the party conducted a campaign around the demand for federal troops to solve the problem of Black defense in the South. For several issues, *The Militant* pounded away at solving the Birmingham crisis through federal troops, but at the height of the crisis, the paper, without any warning, switched to "Arm the Blacks"—a welcome if abrupt development.

The politics and propaganda of the SWP are deliberately noninterventionist. The party proclaims, in effect, that it has no theoretical obligation to go any further.

## Organization and cadre

*Campaigns*

*The Militant* overcompensates for its abstention from the ideological life of the Black community by maintaining a constant agitational fever over "the struggle." This agitation, which should be primarily directed toward white workers, is sent instead into the ghetto, where the need and demand are for political analysis and a program. The ghetto, however, happens to be the only mass market for socialist literature.

In days gone by, *The Militant* was an effective propaganda organ in the ghetto. It was often the only paper endorsing a then unrespected cause, and this gained it enthusiastic support and a foundation for organizational growth. As support for civil rights became more general among whites, even receiving official sanction, the fact that *The Militant* had little to say about the intense theoretical and political inner struggle of the movement nullified its revolutionary stature and made it just another white-supporters paper.

*Mass organizations*

The NAACP's loss of the exclusive franchise on organization and the emergence of a host of more viable rivals broke the old spell cast by the NAACP on the SWP. Even so, our comrades still appear to be restricted in the scope of the area open to them for probing, experimenting and generally intervening as initiators, members, etc. The bewildering Committee to Aid the Monroe Defendants (CAMD) and Monroe Defense Committee (MDC)[42] split indicates a continuing tactical rigidity.

*Recruitment and assimilation*

The record of the party over a 25-year span shows an initial record of brilliant and qualitatively high recruitment, but with little or no assimilation of the Black members into the party.

This is followed by slower and slower rates of recruitment and even less assimilation.

The stream becomes a trickle and then, as the Black struggle reaches its highest point in decades, virtually stops.

## The source

### Trotsky and the Black struggle

The SWP leadership, seeking a doctrinaire explanation of its political failures in the Black struggle, promotes the concept that, as long as it maintains good relations with self-determination, it is politically correct and upholds the tradition of Trotsky. This approach is enforced by regular republication of Trotsky's transcribed and uncorrected conversations on self-determination.

The leadership, however, seeking to recreate Trotsky in their own image, selects only those quotes that serve their purpose. More relevant to the current situation of the party is a letter to Claude McKay, written in 1923:

> In North America the matter is further complicated by the abominable obtuseness and caste presumption of the privileged upper strata of the working class itself, who refuse to recognize fellow workers and fighting comrades in the Negroes. Gompers' policy is founded on the exploitation of such despicable prejudices, and is at the present time the most effective guarantee for the successful subjugation of white and colored workers alike. The fight against this policy must be taken from different sides... One of the most important branches of this conflict consists in enlightening the proletarian consciousness...among the Negro slaves of American capitalism. As stated above, this work can only be carried out by self-sacrificing and politically educated revolutionary Negroes.

> Needless to say, the work is not to be carried on in a spirit of Negro chauvinism which would then merely form a counterpart of white chauvinism, but in a spirit of solidarity of all exploited, without consideration of color.[43]

In a 1932 letter to the International Secretariat (copy to the National Committee of the Communist League of America), Trotsky wrote:

> The difference in our attitude to a petty-bourgeois group and to the proletarian group does not require any explanation. But if a proletarian group functions in an area

*C.L.R. James, West Indian author and SWP member, urged Leon Trotsky to support the demand for Black equality rather than self-determination, which is a slogan appropriate to oppressed nations.*

where the workers are of different races, and in spite of this, remains composed solely of workers of a privileged nationality, then I am inclined to view them with suspicion. Are we not dealing perhaps with the labor aristocracy? Isn't the group infected with slave-holding prejudices, active or passive?[44]

From the above-quoted passages, is there any doubt as to what Trotsky's approach to the question of Blacks and the SWP would be today? He would disdain to discuss the merits of this or that theoretical question until he inquired into the political-sociological reasons for the party's inability to maintain the allegiance of its oppressed-race members.

Trotsky would have solicited the judgment of a thousand radical Blacks who have been in and out of the party over the past 25 years. Neither theoretical discussion nor the adoption of resolutions will take on living meaning unless the opinions and feelings and attitudes of these Blacks (and the thousands of Blacks in and out of the CP as well) have been stated, understood, evaluated and the results incorporated into the daily life of the party.

## Black nationalists in the Marxist movement

The attitude of some of the few Black members still left in the SWP was expressed by Comrade Robert Vernon in his Internal Bulletin, "Why White Radicals Are Incapable of Understanding Black Nationalism," presented to the 1963 pre-convention discussion of the party.[45]

He contended that the SWP can never understand or have significant relations with even radical Blacks because it is comfortable and at home in a world which is alien to the Black and which the Black despises—the world of white America, whose general cultural attitudes are reflected in the SWP. It is right and proper that this should be, he wrote (with superbly objective resignation), for it is the duty of white revolutionaries not to become isolated from the white working class which is going to make the revolution.

Vernon is both stunningly right and fortunately wrong. He is right in his enumeration of the qualities estranging Blacks from the party, but he is wrong in thinking bad politics and confusion are good socialist tactics.

The party *is* isolated from the white working class. It has been isolated primarily because of its revolutionary program and principles. This results from objective conditions over which the party has no control and no amount of conformity to cultural mores or anything else will compensate for it. This isolation will prevail until objective conditions force a change in workingclass opinion. However, the party's concessions to the general illiberal folkways of white America do estrange it from its key victims—Blacks, women, youth—leaving it very isolated indeed.

Former Comrade Johnson [C.L.R. James][46] often said that the inadequacy of white radicals "is not a matter of prejudice, it is a political question." Taking this as a clue, *what* political question?

## Blacks in relation to the working class

It would be impossible to encourage separatism given a realization of how it would affect the proletariat.

What, for example, would the working class in the auto industry do if all Blacks marched back to Africa or off to somewhere else? As SWP advocates of the right of self-determination, we would be obliged to support, help, and theoretically justify this decision. But in the process, key sections of the proletariat might very well become enervated, deprived of their most conscious and militant sector, and rendered incapable of a struggle for socialism for an indefinite historical era. They could well become a prey of fascism.

Posing the matter positively, the Black Question is the *key* question for the proletariat. It is more important to the working class than the trade union question itself, because Black workers carry the key to effective trade unionism. Independent labor political action can be accomplished only through *class consciousness,* which, in turn, can only be realized through the destruction of race-conscious white supremacy.

The IWW used to say that the Black Question was a class question, but actually the converse of this is true: *the class question is in large measure the Black Question.* The class question funnels into and concentrates around the Black issue.

What else explains the fact that 200 years of American history—politics, wars, union organization, domestic turmoil, culture—revolve around this issue? That the very survival of American civilization depends upon the outcome of the struggle for Black equality is taken for granted by militant Black leaders, who, furthermore, warn white America that Blacks will not stop at "civil rights" but will pull the white masses with them as they ascend to real freedom.

When the SWP recognizes the Black struggle as the core ingredient of U.S. history, politics and labor, the SWP then will understand both the proletariat and Blacks a little better.

## The future

What are the tasks of the Socialist Worker's Party in relation to the Black struggle?

### Theoretical

The central theoretical responsibility of the revolutionary party is to reawaken, by example and invitation, Black Marxist scholarship on the Black Question, helping to reverse the "anti-Black-history" attitude among intellectuals described by E.F. Frazier as "escape [from] the Negro heritage."

After years of quiescence, a renaissance is in the making, and the party should both pioneer and encourage it.

Black intellectuals will return to the Black Question if Black militants demand it of them. This process will resurrect the real identity of Blacks, uncovering the truth of their African past and its relation to them today, and rediscovering their heroic past in the U.S.

This reawakening will occur under the ideological auspices of *Revolutionary Integration,* as opposed to nationalism, separatism, reformist integration and pragmatism. Revolutionary Marxists shall not advocate integration into the "burning house" status quo. Integration into a revolution is the answer to "Freedom for what?"

A fundamental aim of the revival-of-theory process will be to convince the Black vanguard of the fundamentals of materialism, which begin with the proposition that *ideas have no color.* Marxism can be utilized by Blacks for their liberation, and in the land of the most powerful capitalists on earth, no other weapon will be adequate.

### Programmatic

The party should first of all become the leading representative of the southern struggle, projecting an extensive propaganda campaign on its behalf.

1. The SWP should cement and broaden the united front

of the northern Black community in defense of the southern struggle.

2. The SWP should elaborate a program designed to publicize the illegal and lawless character of the southern regime, and provide transitional slogans aimed toward its destruction.

Central to the southern struggle is the demand upon Congress that southern congressmen be denied their seats on the grounds that they do not represent legal state governments but a regime imposed after violent overthrow of legal authority and maintained for nearly a century by force and violence.[47]

3. Some derivative demands can be worked out along the following lines:

• After having unseated the southern congressmen, Congress shall take the responsibility for the administration (or for designating an administration) of these areas, pending the establishment of legal democratic governments.

• All armed forces under the jurisdiction of present state governments, including local police and sheriffs' bodies, shall be disbanded and disarmed.

• A volunteer militia shall be recruited from amongst those who support the U.S. Constitution.

• Governments shall be formed under authority of Congress and supervision of the militias on the basis of universal suffrage of all persons over 18 years of age.

The use of this program in arenas such as all election campaigns, memorials to Congress, and threatened injunctions would go a long way toward legalizing the southern revolution. It also would polarize Blacks and their allies on one side, and the capitalist parties on the other, creating a severe crisis in the political system.

## Education

The key to improvement of SWP relations with the Black

movement, given a correct theoretical and political foundation, is knowledge of how to intervene politically in it.

*The Militant* must take the lead in this by correcting its reportorial-agitational approach to civil rights. To the job of reporting the facts must be added the responsibility of *analysis,* drawing the political lessons of events and taking sides in disputed questions on the basis of *principle.*

Led by the center in these matters, branches and individuals will be able to adjust their approach to local problems, keeping in mind Comrade Vernon's advice: that white comrades who can see shortcomings of the various Black movements should learn how to make their criticism known to the Blacks involved, utilizing such relations to broaden their general understanding.

Internal education, political work, dissemination of information, and experience in the Black struggle should become a central concern of the party. This work should be centrally organized and coordinated by Black comrades.

## Tactics and organization

How is such a theoretical and political program to be implemented?

Some of it could be accomplished through the press and organization as it exists today. But other aspects cannot be properly handled by a white party. This indicates the need to change the racial character of the SWP. Can the SWP accomplish this?

*The Black cadre*

The past ten years of struggle have created a large, new, relatively youthful Black cadre. These leaders, together with thousands of unaffiliated radical Blacks, comprise a revolutionary reservoir of considerable depth.

A significant number of these militants should be recruited directly to the party now, but Blacks' powerful urge to independence because of distrust of white radical parties makes recruitment difficult to accomplish. Nevertheless, the primary task, without which all other proposals are meaningless, is to organize this Black vanguard under the banner of socialism, imbue it with the spirit and science of Marxism, and prepare it for the role Trotsky predicted for it: vanguard of the American working class.

*The Black vanguard*

This task poses a tactical problem: if Blacks will not come to the party, shall it go to them? The only realistic solution is to help create a *Black vanguard movement*. This is the heart of Worthy's proposal to launch an anticapitalist Freedom Party.

Such an organization, essential for guiding the southern struggle towards a mass political phase, would be the most dynamic political development of this era. It would have many characteristics of the future mass party of socialism and would be able to fight on all the issues of the day, from local police brutality to defense of the colonial revolution. It would be able to develop the theoretical discussion of the Black Question within the Black community.

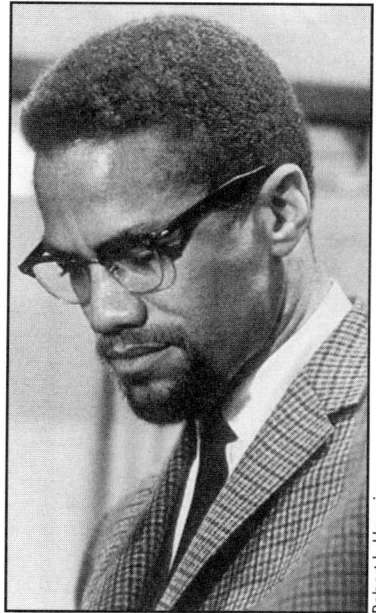

Robert L. Haggins

*Revolutionary leader Malcolm X was moving toward an internationalist and socialist perspective when he was gunned down in 1965.*

There is plenty of room for the entire party membership to participate politically and organizationally in the Black movement, be it independent, integrated, separatist, ambiguous, or racially exclusive. These movements need Marxism to illuminate their problems with theory. They need Bolshevism to advise on the political struggle. And they need Trotskyism to teach the strategy of revolution.

This can be done in political campaigns, in day to day propaganda, in the theoretical magazine, and individually by any comrade who sees that the Black Question is the key question of the American revolution and who will take the time to learn about it before trying to teach.

## Trade union work

Central to work among Blacks is the regrouping of Black and white radicals in the unions, the indispensable starting point of the future left wing. Questions of policy must be carefully thought out, and here the advice and recommendations of the Black comrades to white trade unionists are critical.

White unionists are not required to be silent on all questions pertaining to the Black struggle until "the Blacks have spoken." On certain questions, the white worker must know the precise opinions of at least the leading Blacks before projecting a policy. On others, the white worker must take the initiative.

Examples of the two aspects of white involvement are Black representation and white seniority.

In the fight for representation, Blacks must take the lead, unless exceptional circumstances dictate differently. In the first place, Blacks sometimes prefer to enter this struggle in the concrete, i.e., trying to elect a Black person to a given post without reference to the need for Black representation. We must be sensitive to their desires in such matters. On the other hand, there are many circumstances where Blacks may not want representation, and for good reasons. Like many white members, they do not want to take responsibility for class-collaborationist unionism.

In the fight against the unfair seniority system, white radicals must take the lead. They are the beneficiaries of the racial character of seniority, and it would be wrong for them to sit back and demand that Blacks take the initiative in remedying it. Given the defensive attitude of the union leadership and the central preoccupation of so many unions with defending seniority per se against employers, few workers will push the demand to alter the seniority system. However, radical white workers can address themselves effectively to the issue by citing the injustices, indicating various ways it could be adjusted, and proposing the six-hour day as a way of ameliorating the racial effects of layoff.

• • •

The myth of the nationhood of U.S. Blacks and the corollary right of self-determination will continue to haunt the radical movement until the SWP issues a clear statement on the basically integrationist nature of the Black struggle for equality.

The traditional respect earned by the party for its theoretical precision has been gradually dissipated over the years as the theme of "remaining neutral until the Black people have spoken" carries it further and further away from the living movement, rendering Marxism incomprehensible to Blacks and Blacks incomprehensible to Marxists.

It may be that Blacks will succeed in impressing the SWP with the truth of the problem. Even non-Marxists close to the moods and needs of their race, and familiar with the white radical's habit of operating from *a priori* positions, might manage to unmask the flaws of such reasoning in a sufficiently forceful manner to shake the party out of its complacency.

Still, it would be infinitely preferable for the party to be able to resolve the dilemma without pressure from outside. The unique Black struggle is the most serious test of the SWP's ability to Americanize Marxism, and it would be gratifying if the party could solve the political problems involved in this revolutionary struggle under its own initiative and through its own internal powers.

# 2. Revolutionary Integration: Yesterday and Today

*This groundbreaking resolution on the U.S. Black struggle was adopted by the July 4, 1982 National Convention of the Freedom Socialist Party. It was written by Tom Boot on behalf of the FSP National Committee.*

## Overview

Revolutionary Integration is the theoretical/programmatic position of the Freedom Socialist Party on the Black Question in the United States.

Adopted from the original Richard Fraser/Seattle SWP resolution presented at the Socialist Workers Party national convention in 1963, Revolutionary Integration has profound political implications for the Black movement today—just as it always has in the past. It represents a continuous contemporary thread in the ideological fabric of international Permanent Revolution, the uninterruptible march of all the world's oppressed, led by the working class, toward social, political, and economic equality.

Revolutionary Integration is a precise theory that was arrived at through Marxist method, through a historical analysis of the economic, political, social, and cultural roots of the race system in the United States. It is a scientific and a living answer to the long-standing and acrimonious debate in the radical movement on the question of Black liberation: assimilation vs. nationalism/separatism as the correct and indicated road to freedom.

It is also the answer to the pragmatic what-the-hell, let's-see-what-develops school of "thought."

Revolutionary Integration is the theory that flows from, and is deeply centered in, the day-to-day reality of the U.S. Black struggle.

And it demonstrates that the paramount historic direction of the Black freedom movement has always been toward integration. This primary thrust for integration has been connected to the quest for revolution, and *not* for assimilation into white bourgeois, racist, capitalist, and imperialist America.

## Premises

Revolutionary Integration rests on five basic premises:

1. Blacks are an oppressed *race,* not a nation.

The unscientific concept of "race," based solely on the skin color of sectors of the human race, is a unique social phenomenon created by capitalism to justify the institutions of slavery and oppression through forced segregation and super-exploitation.

2. Racism and race segregation are *fundamental* and *permanent* features of U.S. capitalism as a whole, not just in the South.

The struggle against racism always becomes a fatal dagger pointed at the heart of capitalist power.

3. The main historical direction of the Black movement has been revolt against slavery, segregation, and discrimination. Despite periodic bursts of intensity, separatism has been a *minor and subordinate* current. It is the result of defeats and despair.

4. Blacks and the Black struggle are *key* to the American class struggle and the American revolution. Hence,

Blacks are destined to once again be prime movers in the revolutionary leadership.

The Black struggle is also a decisive *international* question, encompassing the struggle of Africans and other dark-skinned peoples.

5. The task of the Marxist party in the U.S. is to study, participate in, and impact the Black movement, and to develop a cohesive class analysis and decisive program.

A true vanguard party does not capitulate to reactionary and hostile fashions in Black theory and politics, but seeks to provide ideological, political, organizational, and agitational leadership on the Black Question within the party, to our audiences, and to the Black movement itself.

## The present conjuncture

The theory of Revolutionary Integration, as first presented in 1963, was the cumulative response to years of political crisis in the Black struggle.

The Black movement in '63 was on the threshold of a new stage: a stage of orientation toward and organization for social revolution. A showdown with the southern police state was already under way.

But the Black movement lacked four critical elements for success:

1. A politically radical leadership prepared to lead revolutionary work.

2. A developed revolutionary strategy and program.

3. A well-organized and mass-based radical party.

4. A solid alliance with northern labor and the radical movement.

At the dawn of its revolution, the great Black movement of the late '50s, '60s, and early '70s collapsed. The absence of a viable revolutionary *theory* and a bold revolutionary *perspective* derailed it.

An understanding and practical application of the basic

premises of Revolutionary Integration would have profoundly altered the course of Black struggle and recent U.S. history. The Black movement has still to throw off the cloak of passivity, demoralization, and relative paralysis that it donned as the enormous momentum and gains of the earlier period of protest tragically withered away.

The Black movement today is in an even worse state of leaderlessness than it was in the early '50s.

Black struggle, however, has endured for more than two centuries as a *consistent thread of revolt.* It has proceeded in staggering qualitative and quantitative leaps, only to be catapulted backwards by reactionary social winds and forces. These retreats necessitate sifting through the mistakes made in order to arrive at valuable lessons.

Erisa Moore, Black poet, in her 1976 poem "The Bicentennial Celebration-Aberration," writes:

Since construction and renaissance few fought for
   liberation,
It was as though some were dead and some in
   hibernation,
But furious burning memories of your "peculiar
   institution,"
Gave us strength, born of suffering, to attempt a
   resolution—
The 'sixties proved we have determination.[48]

Despite its seemingly dormant state, the Black community today is pervaded with an angry climate. Blacks are under a total economic and social siege unleashed by the frightened and ruthless U.S. ruling class. Black freedom has yet to be won. But how? And to what?

Revolutionary Integration remains the only sensible, realistic, and tested solution. It is the only approach that excites, that engenders a mass responsiveness, that mobilizes, and that conveys a direction and course. That is why clear exposition of Revolutionary Integration by the FSP, and constant discussion of it through public examination and debate, is searingly relevant, instructive, meaningful, and necessary to the Black community.

This present document will examine the theory in the light of recent events and show how it is vindicated by life.

## The Comintern addresses the Black Question

The initial intervention of U.S. radicals into a study of the Black freedom struggle stemmed from the tremendous influence of the Russian Revolution and Bolshevik insistence on the importance of the "most oppressed."

As James P. Cannon wrote in 1962:

> ...Lenin and the Bolsheviks were distinguished from all other tendencies in the...movement by their concern with the problems of oppressed nations and national minorities, and affirmative support...to all "people without equal rights" sincerely and earnestly...They also recognized the great revolutionary potential in the situation of oppressed people and nations, and saw them as important allies of the international working class in the revolutionary struggle against capitalism.[49]

Prior to the Russian Revolution, the alliance of American radicals with Blacks was generally restricted to the workplace.

The Black workers' struggle was deemed to be an economic issue only, part of the class struggle. Radical whites tended to be colorblind, abstaining from the question of the *racial and unique* aspect of the Black problem. To them, workers were workers; race, nationality, and sex were immaterial.

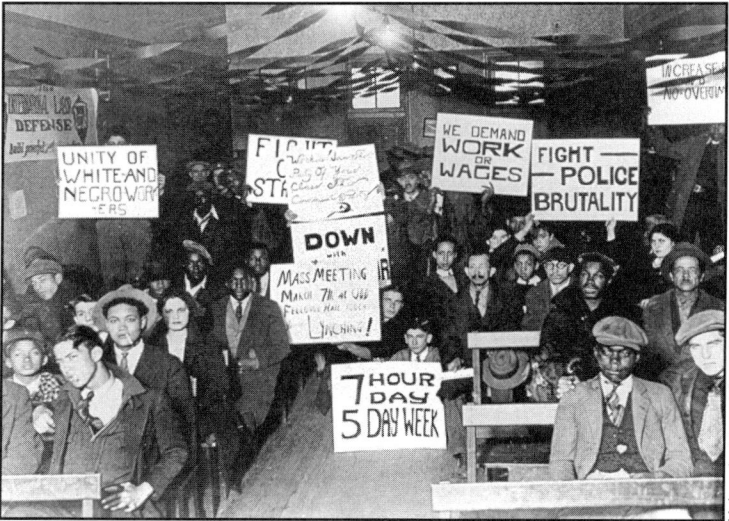

*Groundbreaking cross-racial solidarity at a Communist Party meeting to build Black and white unity, c. 1935. The CP eventually took a nationalist line, but it built important early alliances between African Americans and white labor activists.*

The Industrial Workers of the World (IWW) had an "open-door" membership policy, regardless of race, color, or creed. They sought "industrial" rather than craft organizing, and did not discriminate. Neither did they pay any special attention to workers of color.

But the predominant American Federation of Labor (AFL) craft unions, with only a few exceptions, were Jim Crow. Blacks were either in separate locals or unorganized.

The Socialist Party (SP) platform included no special planks on the Black Question, and considered the plight of Black workers on the same scale as that of whites—a simple struggle between workers and bosses. The programmatic solution for both was "salvation through socialism."

This abstention on the Black Question by the U.S. Left reflected the pervasiveness of institutionalized racism, and provided a convenient cover for the subconscious, underlying racial prejudice of white workers and white radicals.

## A special question

The Bolsheviks were different. According to Cannon:

> The Russians in the Comintern started on the American communists with the harsh, insistent demand that they shake off their own unspoken prejudices, pay attention to the special problems and grievances of the American Negroes, go to work among them, and champion their cause in the white community.[50]

The Comintern (Communist International) was formed in March 1919 through the leadership of the Russian Bolsheviks. Also known as the Third International, it represented the third attempt to build an international revolutionary workingclass organization that could coordinate revolutionary struggle worldwide and provide ideological and material aid to national sections throughout the world in making their own revolutions.[51]

Through Lenin's leadership in the early 1920s, the Comintern established that the Black Question was a *special question*, that it involved *doubly exploited* second-class citizens, and required *special demands* to be incorporated into the overall revolutionary program.

The infant American Communist Party, to its credit, accepted this historic mandate in the 1920s. Its view of the Black Question as a special problem distinguished the party from the IWW and the SP, solidified the developing bond with the Comintern, and charted a new course on the revolutionary map for the international proletariat, which was called upon to support the fight for Black equality.

The CP immediately proposed an alliance between Blacks and the labor movement. William Z. Foster, the

Communist labor leader, organized the Trade Union Educational League (TUEL) in 1924. TUEL sought to unite communists, radicals, and moderates within the AFL to change its craft-based structure.

Said TUEL, in its 1924 program on the Black struggle:

> The problem of the political and industrial disfranchised Negroes shall occupy the serious attention of the League. The League shall demand that the Negroes be given the same social, political and industrial rights as whites, including the right to work in all trades, equal wages, admission to all trade unions, abolition of Jim-Crow cars and restaurants.[52]

## The Second Congress, 1920

At the Second Congress of the Comintern, John Reed initiated a preliminary discussion of the Black Question.

A section of the "Preliminary Draft Theses on the National and Colonial Question," written by Lenin for the conference, had stated:

> ...it is necessary for the Communist Parties to render direct aid to the revolutionary movements in the dependent and subject nations (for example, in Ireland, the Negroes in America, etc.) and in the colonies.[53]

Reed, a member of the U.S. delegation to the Congress, presented an excellent summary of the Black struggle and the history of U.S. racism. *Reed proffered his own opinions on the question.* His position differed from Lenin's nationalist view of Blacks, essentially amounting to Revolutionary Integration:

> As an oppressed and downtrodden people, the Negro offers to us a twofold opportunity: first, a strong

race and social movement; second, a strong proletarian labor movement... In both the northern and southern parts of the country, the one aim must be to unite the Negro and the white laborer in common labor unions; this is the best and the quickest way to destroy race prejudice and develop class solidarity.[54]

A lively debate ensued at the Congress over whether Blacks constituted a nation.

Lenin did not arrive at a firm decision on Black nationhood, nor did he propose a slogan for Black self-determination; he lacked the necessary specific information on the situation and had not studied the American race system. But he urged the Congress to allocate a definite period of time for thorough study and debate on the question.

Lenin's invaluable contribution to the international struggles of specially oppressed peoples—in addition to his great work on the national and colonial questions—was his insistence on *the vanguard political role of the most oppressed.* Trotsky always gave him credit for developing this strategy.

In the preface to the first translation into Afrikaans of *The Communist Manifesto,* published in 1937 on its 90th anniversary, Trotsky wrote:

> The Communists, declares the *Manifesto,* everywhere support every revolutionary movement against the existing social and political order of things. The movement of the colored races against their imperialist oppressors is one of the most important and powerful movements against the existing order and therefore calls for the complete, unconditional and unlimited support on the part of the proletariat. Credit for the revolutionary strategy of oppressed nationalities belongs primarily to Lenin.[55]

REVOLUTIONARY INTEGRATION

Revolutionary Integration has thoroughly absorbed this concept. As stated in the 1963 resolution:

> That Blacks should lead white workers in social awareness, militancy, and class solidarity is an illustration of the vanguard role they play.[56]

## The Fourth Congress, 1922

The Fourth Congress of the Communist International, under Lenin's leadership, adopted theses on the oppression of Black people worldwide. Said the "Theses":

> The penetration and intensive colonization of the areas inhabited by the black races is the last great problem on the solution of which the further development of capitalism itself depends.[57]

In a spirit of internationalism, the document continues:

> ...the history of the Negroes in America qualifies them to play an important part in the liberation struggle of the entire African race...[58]

The document extols the international solidarity of the most oppressed, and outlines the tasks for Bolsheviks:

> It is the task of the Communist International to bring home to the Negroes that they are not the only people suffering from the oppression of imperialism and capitalism, that the workers and peasants of Europe, Asia, and America are also victims of the imperialist exploiter, that in India and China, in Persia and Turkey, in Egypt and Morocco the oppressed colored workers are defending themselves heroically against the imperialist exploiters, that these peoples are revolting against

the same intolerable conditions which drive the Negroes themselves to desperation—racial oppression, social and economic inequality, intense industrial exploitation; that these peoples are fighting for the same objects as the Negroes—political, economic and social emancipation and equality.[59]

The Fourth Congress adopted the following active program:

> 1. ...support...every form of the Negro movement which undermines or weakens capitalism...

> 2. ...fight for the equality of the white and black races, for equal wages and equal political and social rights.

> 3. ...use every means...to force the trade unions to admit black workers...or to conduct special propaganda for the entry of Negroes into the unions. If this should prove impossible, the Communist International will organize the Negroes in trade unions of their own and use united front tactics to compel their admission.[60]

The final act of the Congress was a motion to take immediate steps to convene a World Negro Congress to advance the struggle.

The discussion of the Black Question was well under way—a tremendous step forward in the age of Permanent Revolution!

## Lenin on the national/colonial question

Lenin was firmly convinced, especially following World War I, that the key to toppling national bourgeois structures in oppressor countries lay in the power of national minorities to unshackle their colonial chains.

At the Second Congress of the International in 1920, Lenin had presented his preliminary thesis on the "National and Colonial Question"—the unchallengeable right of oppressed nations to self-determination.

The Comintern's adoption of this thesis was a mandate to all Bolsheviks: actively assist in the liberation of all nationally oppressed minorities. Lenin's concept remains a programmatic legacy for international class struggle and a decisive part of the theory of Permanent Revolution.

The Bolshevik definition of a nation was enumerated by Stalin in his only theoretical work, a book inspired by and closely edited by Lenin. A nation is "an historically evolved, stable community of people formed on the basis of a common language, territory, economic life, and psychological makeup manifested in a common culture." Stalin elaborated as follows:

> It must be emphasized that none of the above characteristics is by itself sufficient to define a nation... It is sufficient for a single one of these characteristics to be absent and the nation ceases to be a nation... It is possible to conceive of people possessing a common "national character," but they cannot be said to constitute a single nation if they are economically disunited, inhabit different territories, speak different languages.[61]

As Megan Cornish of the FSP wrote in her 1978 resolution, "The National Question in the U.S.," "it is the *totality of the 'condition of life,'* the 'living social, economic, and cultural environment' surrounding oppressed groups that determines their character."[62]

The precision and firmness of Lenin's definition of a nation is critical. A nation has particular rights and inevitably advances particular demands *not applicable to a non-*

*nation!* An oppressed nationality *inherently* has the right to self-determination, the right to decide its own political course, the right to separate from and defeat the oppressor nation.

Cornish writes:

As contemporary developing nations come to life, they are already under the thumb of advanced imperialist nations. It is the responsibility of the internationalists to recognize the validity of the democratic right of nations to liberation from the oppressor nation. The right of nations to self-determination, therefore, is the crux of Lenin's policy toward oppressed nations.[63]

Lenin explained the right to self-determination as follows:

...exclusively the right to independence in the political sense, the right to free political separation from the oppressor nation. Specifically, this demand for political democracy implies complete freedom to agitate for secession and for a referendum on secession by the seceding nation. This demand, therefore, is not the equivalent of a demand for separation, fragmentation, and the formation of smaller states. It implies only a consistent expression of struggle against all national oppression.[64]

The right of self-determination is a democratic right. It cannot be denied. However, the purpose of raising the slogan is to further *class struggle*. In the event that secession/separation is determined to be reactionary, regressive, and injurious to class struggle, it is the responsibility of Marxists not only to support the *right* of self-determination but to mount at the same time a public and vigilant *opposition* to a policy of separation. Oppressed nations have the right to determine whether or not they want to separate, and the party has the right and responsibility to make its *opinion* clear. The party is free to oppose separation; it is not free to oppose a referendum to decide the issue.

Lenin's approach was ever specific, concrete, and *political.* Self-determination was a slogan and an act that jointly served the needs of oppressed nations *and* general revolutionary expediency. But after his death in 1924, Comintern policy on colonial nations and on the Black struggle deteriorated, and detoured into mechanistic and opportunistic channels.

## Stalin's Black Belt dictum

That special World Negro Congress called for by the Comintern in 1922 was never held.

Following Lenin's death in 1924, Stalin consolidated his control of the Soviet bureaucracy. He replaced Lenin and Trotsky's internationalism with the absurd ideology of "Socialism in One Country," and he proceeded to systematically destroy Bolshevism, the party, workers' democracy, and Soviet social gains. Trotsky and his co-thinkers organized the Left Opposition as a faction within the party and the International, and were soon exiled, murdered, or forced to capitulate. "Darkness at Noon" was at hand.

At the Sixth Congress of the Comintern held in Moscow in the summer of 1928, Cannon and other members of the American CP read Trotsky's criticism of the draft program of the Comintern—a document written by the expelled leader and circulated at the congress before it could be suppressed.

The document's critical analysis of Stalinism cleared up all doubts for the Americans; they returned home and began organizing a Left Opposition in their own party. By October 1928, they had been expelled from the American CP.

However, Cannon and other adherents of the Left Opposition refused to recognize their expulsion and continued to work as a faction of the CP. They formalized their grouping as the Communist League of America, affiliated with the International Left Opposition.

In 1928, the Communist International also adopted a brand new position on the Black Question. The Comintern pontifically announced a policy of *self-determination for the U.S. Black Belt*. They had arbitrarily decided that Blacks in the U.S. conformed to the criteria of a nation and should therefore fight for a nation and for the right of self-determination in the southern "Black Belt" states with majority Black populations.

The Comintern never consulted American Blacks or the U.S. Communist Party before adopting and internationally publicizing this position. Nevertheless, the American CP blithely announced support of the Black Belt thesis. "The Communists," they said, "are for a Negro Republic."

They immediately began to advocate this position within the radical and labor movements, and later in the CIO organizing campaign.

*But what about the twelve million Blacks in America?* What did *they* advocate, think, want? They would be directly affected by this policy of "self-chosen" segregation imposed on them by the influential CP.

As Lenin had stated, the principle of self-determination specifically granted the right of an oppressed national movement to choose or reject separation. Did Black Americans *want* a nation? And, first and foremost: *Were Blacks a nation, and if so, by what and by whom was this determined?*

The Stalinists said Blacks were a nation; the Comintern now knew more about Blacks than Blacks knew about themselves. This deliberate revision of Lenin's careful precepts on how to proceed on the National Question placed

Stalin and the International squarely in the league of the bureaucratic paternalists. Without scholarship, or investigation, or consultation, the Comintern still knew what was best for the souls of Black folk.

*In 1931, the Communist Party launched an international defense of nine Black youths framed on rape charges in Scottsboro, Alabama. The CP later agreed to a disastrous plea-bargain deal in the interests of U.S.-Moscow cooperation.*

To this day, world Stalinism clings to Black nationalism in the United States. Decades of CP scholarship (Herbert Aptheker, etc.) have been devoted to proving that a separate Black state in the South is the solution to racial horror. Angela Davis skirts and evades the issue, but it is implicit, if no longer clearly defined, in CP theoretical work.

The issue became moot in practice, of course, following the vast Black migration out of the South during World War II, followed by the ferocious battles for social *integration* mounted by the Montgomery bus boycott, Martin Luther King, Jr., the Student Non-Violent Coordinating Committee (SNCC), the Mississippi Freedom Democratic Party, the Black Panthers, and scores of activists and organizations in the late '50s and the '60s. Today, the CP plays it both ways, like the SWP does, bending their line depending on whom they are addressing!

## Debate in the Fourth International

The Communist League of America (CLA) held its first national conference in 1928. Trotsky, exiled by Stalin to Prinkipo, Turkey, corresponded with his American co-thinkers, expressing his views in "Tasks of the American Opposition."

Among the primary issues addressed was the crucial importance of the Black Question. Said Trotsky:

> The trade union bureaucrats, like the bureaucrats of false Communism, live in the atmosphere of aristocratic prejudices of the upper strata of the workers. It will be a tragedy if the Oppositionists are infected even in the slightest degree with these qualities. We must not only reject and condemn these prejudices; we must burn them out of our consciousness to the last trace. We must find the road to the most deprived, to the

darkest strata of the proletariat, beginning with the Negro, whom capitalist society has converted into a pariah and who must learn to see in us his revolutionary brothers. And this depends wholly upon our energy and devotion to the work.[65]

The CLA, as a result of its knowledge of and intervention into the Black struggle, did not perceive the struggle as nationalist. Faced with the Black Belt thesis of the CP, the League said that while they did not contest the right of Blacks to self-determination, they still firmly advocated the position that self-determination was not the issue around which the *majority* of the Black proletariat, sharecroppers, and farmers could be mobilized for struggle.

The CLA rightly feared that the slogan of self-determination for the Black populace would be regressive rather than progressive. Unconfident and unclear on the issues, however, they hadn't yet reached the point of formulating their theoretical position against it.

### The Trotsky-Swabeck discussion, 1933

Arne Swabeck of the CLA met with Trotsky in Prinkipo in 1933. Placed on the uppermost level of their discussion agenda was "The Negro Question in America."

Swabeck represented the majority opinion of the CLA on the Black Question. He stated to Trotsky:

We have in this question within the American League no noticeable differences of important character, nor have we yet formulated a program. I present therefore, only the view which we have developed in general.

How must we view the position of the American Negro: As a national minority or a racial minority? This is of the greatest importance for our program...

The Negroes have become fully assimilated, Americanized, and their life in America has overbalanced the traditions of the past, modified and changed them. We cannot consider the Negroes a national minority in the sense of having their own separate language. They have no special national customs, or special national culture or religion; nor have they any special national minority interests. It is impossible to speak of them as a national minority in this sense. It is therefore our opinion that the American Negroes are a racial minority whose position and interests as such are subordinated to the class relations of the country and depending upon them...

But we contest the correctness of the slogan of "self-determination" as a means to win the Negro masses. The impulse of the Negro population is first of all in the direction toward equality in a social, political and economic sense.[66]

Swabeck explained that the Black Belt thesis appealed mostly to the Black petty-bourgeoisie. The CLA feared that this slogan placed the petty-bourgeoisie ahead of Black workers in the order of political importance.

...the poor farmers and sharecroppers are the closest allies of the proletariat, but it is our opinion that they can be won as such mainly on the basis of the class struggle.[67]

Trotsky responded by explaining that he had not had the opportunity for an in-depth study of U.S. race relations, but that the Black Question was of the utmost importance. His views were based only upon general considerations. Said Trotsky:

> ...the Negroes are a race and not a nation: Nations grow out of the racial material under definite conditions... We do, of course, not obligate the Negroes to become a nation; if they are, then that is a question of their consciousness, that is, what they desire and what they strive for.[68]

Trotsky said, however, that he found no reason why the CLA should not advance the demand for self-determination, and that he would "rather lean toward the standpoint of the Communist Party."

Swabeck voiced strong disagreement. He urged Trotsky to consider instead the slogan of Social, Political, and Economic Equality that the League proposed in opposition to the Black Belt slogan. The CLA slogan, Swabeck felt, represented completely the *proletarian* direction of the Black worker.

Trotsky urged the CLA to undertake serious study of the question before formalizing a position). But he left no doubt that the American Question *was* the Black Question.

In a strong admonition to the comrades, he stated:

> It is very possible that the Negroes...will proceed to the proletarian dictatorship in a couple of gigantic strides, ahead of the great bloc of white workers. They will then furnish the vanguard. I am absolutely sure that they will in any case fight better than the white workers. That, however, can happen only provided the Communist party carries on an uncompromising merciless struggle not against the supposed national prepossessions of the Negroes but against the colossal prejudices of the white workers and gives it no concession whatever.[69]

Soon after the 1933 Trotsky-Swabeck discussion, fascism swept Germany. Hitler's Third Reich and the Nazi ideology of white male supremacy came to power, thanks to the suicidal tactics of the virtually mute German Communist Party and the Third International.

The Left Opposition condemned the bankruptcy of the International, manifested by its capitulation to fascism *without a fight*. Trotskyists declared the International moribund and split from it. The CLA publicly declared independence from the American Communist Party and undertook regroupment efforts, fusing with the Workers Party and then entering the Socialist Party.

Merged with the SP left wing, the CLA founded the Socialist Workers Party in 1938 and affiliated with the new Fourth International led by Trotsky.

Hence, the serious discussion that Trotsky had requested on the Black Question was delayed.

## The Trotsky-Johnson discussion, 1939

Consideration of the issue was resumed in discussions preceding the 1939 SWP convention. Trotsky, living in exile in Coyoacan, Mexico, met with a delegation of American comrades including the Black revolutionary intellectual and writer, C.L.R. James, known by his political pen name, J.R. Johnson.

Born in Trinidad, Johnson moved to England in 1932 and became active in the British Trotskyist movement. In 1939, he came to the U.S. and joined the SWP.

In the discussions, Johnson strongly held that in order for Blacks to be won over to socialism, the party must adopt Swabeck's proposed slogan of Social, Political, and Economic Equality.

But, said Johnson, if Blacks want self-determination, then, however reactionary it might be in every other respect, it would be the business of the party to advance the slogan.

He said he hoped that Blacks would *not* want self-determination.

Trotsky again said that to label the consequences of self-determination as reactionary or abstract or wrong was, in his judgment, dangerous. He said that "to fight for the possibility of realizing an independent state is a sign of great moral and political awakening. It would be a tremendous revolutionary step forward."

Johnson, in rebuttal, described the extreme danger in the effects of the slogan. It would shatter the young alliance between Black and white workers in the South, expressed in such forms as the Sharecroppers Union, founded in 1931 at Camp Hill, Alabama.[70]

Johnson said Trotsky placed far more faith in the self-determination slogan than Johnson thought warranted. However, Johnson agreed that the party would remain temporarily neutral on the question.

## The 1939 resolution

The SWP adopted its first *theoretical* position on the Black Question at the second convention of the party in 1939.

The resolution was titled "The Right of Self-Determination and the Negro in the United States of North America."

The general line was adaptation to the direction of the Black struggle, i.e., whatever Blacks decided in the course of their struggle, the party would follow and support.

What did this mean? In essence, although without stating it so clearly, the SWP tail-ended the Communist Party's nationalist line, although much more weakly and cautiously. The SWP did not *decree* separatism—it merely resolved to wait and see.

SWP policy was due to pressure from the CP position, and from Marcus Garvey's "Back to Africa" movement, which had influenced thousands of Blacks. The resolution characterized the situation:

The Garvey movement, one of the most powerful political mass movements ever seen in the USA, concealed behind its fantastic and reactionary slogan of "Back to Africa" the desire (revolutionary in essence) for a Negro state. The Negroes no more desired to go to Africa of their own free will than German Jews before Hitler wanted to go to Palestine. The masses of Negroes, particularly in the South, dominated by the heritage of slavery and the apparently irresistible numbers and state power of the whites, did not dare to raise the slogan of a Black state in America. But in a revolutionary crisis, as they begin to shake off the state coercion and ideological domination of American bourgeois society, their first step may well be to demand the control, both actual and symbolical, of their own future destiny. The question of whether Negroes in America are a national minority to which the slogan of self-determination applies will be solved in practice.[71]

George Breitman, the SWP's expert on the Black movement, commented on this 1939 resolution in the 1963 resolution, "Freedom Now: The New Stage in the Struggle for Negro Emancipation":

> In 1939, we foresaw the possibility that the Negro people, as part of their struggle to end centuries of oppression and exploitation, might some day decide that they want a separate nation, controlled and administered by themselves. We said that if this happened, it would settle the long theoretical dispute about whether or not Negroes are a national minority as well as a racial minority and that we as supporters of the right of self-determination would support the Negro demand for a separate nation and do everything in our power to help them obtain it. In taking this position we did not become

> advocates of a separate nation, as the Communist Party used to be, nor do we advocate it now. What we advocate is the right of the Negro people to decide this question themselves. All we commit ourselves to do is support their fight to achieve whatever they decide they want, whether it be equality through integration or equality through segregation, or both.[72]

What an easy, but treacherous, road for Marxists! What a facile way to escape the hot seat of revolutionary leadership. Sit back and wait for the Blacks to decide and take no position yourself! Leninism this is not.

U.S. Trotskyists, for more than a decade, had essentially adhered to Revolutionary Integration on the Black Question. Their proposed slogan, "Social, Political, and Economic Equality," was a positive step in the correct direction, a Leninist approach of looking to the most oppressed—to Blacks as the vanguard of the American working class.

This was the correct program. And it was the American comrades' responsibility to convince Trotsky, who believed that Blacks were an oppressed race and not *yet* a nation, of the incorrectness of applying the right of self-determination to the Black Question. But they didn't.

Trotsky's enormous authority lent weight to his insistence on the great moral and political awakening that would arise out of the fight for an independent Black state. His feeling that Blacks could and would "become" a nation overshadowed his judgment of the reality, and he applied the slogan of the right to self-determination to American Blacks without continued strong resistance from those who knew better.

His lack of knowledge of U.S. race relations should have been supplemented by firm insistence on and confidence in their own experience by the American comrades. But their early vacillation—and intimidation—on the question

*An African American unit of Army nurses arrives in Scotland in 1944. WWII sparked Black migration from the South, new job opportunities and service in the segregated armed forces. African American nurses worked in exclusively Black wards.*

was the start of the SWP's long road to adaptation, zigzagging, and tail-ending on the Black struggle.

## SWP campaigns for equality

The 1940s brought decisive change to Black Americans.

The depression had ended. A burgeoning war economy opened new employment opportunities—formerly closed to Blacks—in big industry. The labor market needed the extra hands of toilers from the always-accessible pool of unemployed Blacks, other people of color, and women.

Black migration from the South to the North and West accelerated as jobs became available in the auto, steel, and airplane plants, and in the shipyards.

Black women were finally allowed to leave the kitchens and domiciles of white families and head for factories and shops where they quickly showed their proficiency and joined unions.

115

Black men, meanwhile, were being drafted into the segregated armed forces, exhorted to win yet another war for democracy even as conditions on U.S. soil remained on the level of "Whites Only" signs in public restrooms, restaurants, and theatres.

Job availability in the beginning of the decade demanded *mobility,* which in turn changed the demographic distribution of the most important sector of U.S. labor— Black workers. The *workplace,* to a greater degree than ever before, introduced and accelerated integration. White workers met Black workers—in many instances, for the first time—and U.S. society hasn't been the same since.

Racial integration leapt ahead in the '40s. Blacks were upwardly bound, demanding equality. A. Philip Randolph, founder of the Brotherhood of Sleeping Car Porters, was the militant spokesperson for this generation of Black workers.

Once a Socialist Party member, Randolph vehemently advocated alliance of Black and white workers, and demanded an end to Jim Crow laws and to racist discrimination within the AFL. In 1940, he became bitterly angry at the government's discriminatory labor practices in defense industries and in the blatantly segregated armed forces.

President Franklin D. Roosevelt, backed by the Stalinists and liberal patriots, totally rejected the urgent demands of Randolph and Black leaders to immediately end discriminatory practices. Randolph then announced:

> Only power can effect the enforcement and adoption of a given policy. Power is the active principle of only the organized masses, the masses united for definite purpose.[73]

Thus was born the March on Washington Movement, a plan to mobilize thousands of Blacks to march on the nation's capital under the slogan: "We loyal Negro American citizens demand the right to work and fight for our country."

Blacks throughout the country were organized primarily by the Brotherhood of Sleeping Car Porters. The Roosevelt administration, after hurling repeated insults and denigrations at the march organizers, was forced to concede on June 24, 1941, due to fierce public pressure. And Randolph canceled the march!

Roosevelt's concession was the heralded event of the day. He established, in his Presidential Order, that the "policy of the United States...shall be no discrimination in the employment of workers in defense industries or government because of race, creed, color, or national origin..."

To implement this Presidential Order, the Fair Employment Practices Committee (FEPC) was established on July 18, 1941. "Its objective was twofold: (1) to put Negroes and workers from other minority groups into war industry, and (2) to raise the morale of those who suffered from discrimination."[74]

The FEPC challenged discriminatory hiring policies during the war period in the unions and in industry, and remained an important watchdog and interventionist committee against such practices until 1946 when its power became negligible as a result of Truman's lip-service to racial equality.

Despite Roosevelt's capitulation to national pressure and his establishment of the FEPC, Randolph erred when he canceled the March on Washington, and when he heralded Roosevelt's declaration as the "second Emancipation Proclamation."

This was not the first time that Randolph had aborted mass protests and strikes before they came to fruition. He often capitulated to his racist opponents without winning his stated demands.

Under Randolph's leadership, the Sleeping Car Porters in March 1928 voted unanimously to strike the Pullman

Company after its repeated refusal to recognize the union's right to collective bargaining. But in June, Randolph called off the strike without consulting the membership.

Discussing this move by Randolph, labor historian Philip S. Foner quotes from the July 20, 1931 edition of *Liberator,* a contemporary Black communist weekly:

> The chances of success were very bright. The rank and file of the porters were very militant. The Randolph leadership and the AF of L called the strike off, betraying Negro workers in the interests of the labor fakers.[75]

Randolph's weakness stemmed from his social democratic politics, which impelled him to concede time and again to class enemies. He was a pacifist (a conscientious objector in his youth) and an adherent of Gandhi's passive resistance techniques.

Randolph was also a red-baiter and virulent anticommunist. French Marxist Daniel Guérin comments:

> The evolution of A. Philip Randolph shows a certain parallel with that of Walter P. Reuther. Both of them trade union leaders, both of them beginning with socialist tendencies, they each made a united front with the Stalinists up to the outbreak of World War II, only to become subsequently their most frenzied enemies.[76]

The Communist Party in 1941 publicly deserted the cause of Black freedom. It admonished Blacks to suppress their grievances in order to win WWII and "defend the Soviet Union" against Nazi Germany's invasion.

The CP's appalling new course, dictated from Moscow, was diametrically opposed to its previous position of total support for the Stalin-Hitler pact signed in 1939. Members shamelessly whipped up patriotic war hysteria, frenziedly promoted labor's heinous no-strike pledge, and deserted their own Black comrades, some of whom were nationally recognized leaders in the fight for Black equality.

The SWP, to its credit, remained steadfast in the fight against Jim Crow throughout the war and postwar period. The party jumped into Black civil rights battles and stayed there. It picked up the slack after the CP dropped out.

Unlike the CP, the party nationally endorsed the March on Washington. And despite the comparative youth, small size, and concentration in the North of the SWP, it became the only, undisputed, and acknowledged white radical organization to champion Black equality in the '40s. It wholeheartedly tackled racist discrimination and segregation and defended Black militants and victims during the war.

Daniel Guérin addressed the divergent positions of the CP and the SWP during this period. He wrote of the SWP:

> Like the CP, it has also unquestionably committed some tactical errors, and its theoretical program on the Negro Question has not always been free of indecisive formulations. But if the SWP has not succeeded in rooting itself among the Negro masses as deeply as its uncompromising attitude against Jim Crow should have made possible, it nonetheless deserves tribute for the consistency and perseverance of its activities. It can be saluted particularly—unlike the CP—for never having abandoned the cause of Negro emancipation in the interests of Russian diplomacy.[77]

In 1931, the Communist Party had mounted a national defense campaign in support of nine Black youths sentenced to death in Scottsboro, Alabama on a phony rape charge. The party's impassioned public work for the acquittal of the "Scottsboro Boys" received international public attention and acclaim. Things chilled, Guérin said,

> ...when the Communist Party, at the Kremlin's in-
> stigation, made the big "People's Front" turn in 1935
> and sacrificed both the labor movement and the Negro
> movement to the interests of promoting an alliance
> between Washington and Moscow. The Stalinist rep-
> resentative on a new Scottsboro Defense Committee
> agreed to a deal with the Jim Crow authorities whereby
> some of the defendants would plead guilty in return for
> letting others go free.[78]

The SWP publicly denounced this opportunistic ploy of
the CP as a sacrifice of Black equality for an illusory bet-
terment of "peaceful and cooperative" relations between
the Kremlin and Washington. Years later, in 1951, the chair-
man of the Scottsboro Defense Committee confirmed the
correctness of the SWP's accusations, according to Guérin.

The SWP was a recognized and respected champion of
the Black cause in the 1940s, and its achievements high-
light a proud chapter in the history of American Trotskyism.

In 1940, the party defended 15 Black sailors from the
U.S.S. Philadelphia who were court-martialed for decrying
the Navy's segregationist policies.

In 1946, the party organized an anti-Klan campaign after a KKK vigilante mob in Fontana, California set fire to
the home of a Black family and killed them all.

In the Midwest, the party conducted a successful defense campaign for a Black worker in Chicago, James
Hickman, who charged that his white landlord purposely
set fire to his home and killed his children.

And in virtually every SWP branch across the country,
the membership fought diligently for racial equality in the
unions, in hiring practices, and in neighborhood housing.
Boycotts, picket lines, protest meetings, and special commit-

tees and alliances were organized or endorsed by the party.
SWPers launched or supported campaigns against racial
prejudice and stereotyping in the media, the movies and
theatre, and in every arena of popular culture. National campaigns and issues championed by the NAACP, CORE, and
local civil rights groups found the party deeply involved.

The SWP's sincere support for Black equality, and its
consistent fight against racist attacks and government repression, cemented a solid alliance with the advanced
Black workers. Writes Guérin:

> The government's efforts to suppress the *Militant*
> during the war were frankly motivated, in part, by the
> SWP's irreconcilable struggle against all forms of white
> supremacy.[79]

By 1948, almost half the party was Black. In some
branches, the majority was Black. And clashes between the
real but hidden position of the SWP central leadership on
Black nationalism, and the public stance on integration and
the militant battle for equality, were breaking out. The clash
took some interesting forms, such as condemnation by
white leaders of interracial marriage and sex relations
within the party, which the Blacks defended.

The hostilities were clear. The party secretly had a *dual*
line, and the secret was showing.

### The 1948 resolution

J.R. Johnson, who had said to Trotsky in 1939 that "The
Negro, fortunately for socialism, does not want self-determination," was the principal author of the 1948 SWP resolution on the Black Question.

Johnson's dramatic thesis described *the dual nature* of
the Black movement: at once an integral part of the class
struggle, *and simultaneously* an independent, supra-class,

*racial* battle for equality.

> The Negro people in all aspects of their social and cultural life are a part of the American people. At the same time it must be recognized that the Negro struggle is not identical with the proletarian movement toward socialism. It exists as a distinct movement of an oppressed minority within the country, possessing its own historical origins, special characteristics, forms of development and methods of action. The economic, political, social and cultural degradation of the Negro people below the levels of even the most exploited layers of the working class places them in an exceptional position and impels them to play an exceptional role within the social structures of American capitalism.[80]

Johnson's sociological analysis was brilliant. But his theoretical conclusion was hedged, ambiguous, subtle. He avoided a definitive answer on the *basic nature* of the Black Question even as he propounded a basically integrationist line.

George Breitman's 1963 summary of the 1948 resolution stated:

> ...we noted that the growing "feeling of racial and national solidarity among the Negro people thus far aims solely at acquiring enough force and momentum to break down the barriers that exclude Negroes from American society, showing few signs of aiming at national separatism." It was clear that the vast majority of the Negroes were integrationist in the sense that they favored abolition of each and every discriminatory and segregationist device and institution in this country. But we did not take that to mean that the Negro masses had

reached a conclusive position for or against separatism. We felt both in 1939 and 1948 that the Negro people might make a different decision about separatism in the future.[81]

What a tragedy—that serious Marxists would not take a definitive position on such an important issue as the character of the Black struggle. Everyone knows that *not* to take a position *is* to take a position. To avoid a position is pure and simple anti-Leninist abstentionism—or refusal to reveal one's real position.

The 1948 convention adopted Johnson's essentially integrationist resolution, which geared up the party to further years of energetic intervention into the movement. Still, the *practice* always contradicted the (hidden) *theory*.

This contradiction was summarized by Clara Fraser in a 1981 Freedom Socialist Party National Committee discussion:

> Fundamentally, the SWP says that Blacks are a nation, or can become a nation, or will vote themselves into a nation, or will take on the appurtenances of a nation— now, that is more than a *concession* to the nationalist theory.[82]

## Emergence of the Revolutionary Integration position

In the early 1950s, opposition formed in the SWP over the confusing line on the Black Question.

A small group of Black, Chicano, and white comrades in Los Angeles began to study the matter in earnest. Most of the subsequent writing was done by Richard Fraser and some of this material was published in internal bulletins.

When Fraser moved to Seattle in 1956, the entire Seattle branch, led by organizer Dan Roberts, endorsed the Los Angeles minority position, now called Revolutionary Integration.

The minority took its cue from the works of the most distinguished Black scholars and analysts. Revolutionary Integration held that Blacks are not a nation, that racism based on skin color is distinct from national oppression, that the prime historic direction of Blacks is toward full equality and integration into the general struggle for social change, and that the Black struggle in America is an essential component of the class struggle, the key question of the American revolution, and the domestic link to the African and world struggles of colonial people.

The minority's position was the antithesis of the SWP doctrine that (1) radicals had to wait until the Black movement gave the green light to a particular direction of struggle, and that (2) Blacks were both an oppressed race and a potential nation.

It was during this period, in 1951, that Daniel Guérin published *Negroes on the March,* a profound theoretical treatise on the Black American struggle.

Intrigued by the contrast of U.S. racism with French colonialism, Guérin lived in America from 1947-48 as an observer and critic of Jim Crow. The basic premises of his work are Revolutionary Integrationist, closely paralleling the ideas of the SWP minority.

*Negroes on the March* states that American racism is rooted in U.S. capitalism and imperialism; that the fight for equality has propelled Blacks toward total assimilation into American society, despite nationalist or chauvinist tendencies within the movement; and that workingclass victory in America will fail without a concrete alliance of the vanguard of Black workers, workers of color, and white workers united to dismantle all vestiges of capitalism:

It is not unreasonable to think that at the end of this evolution the Negroes will actively contribute to the

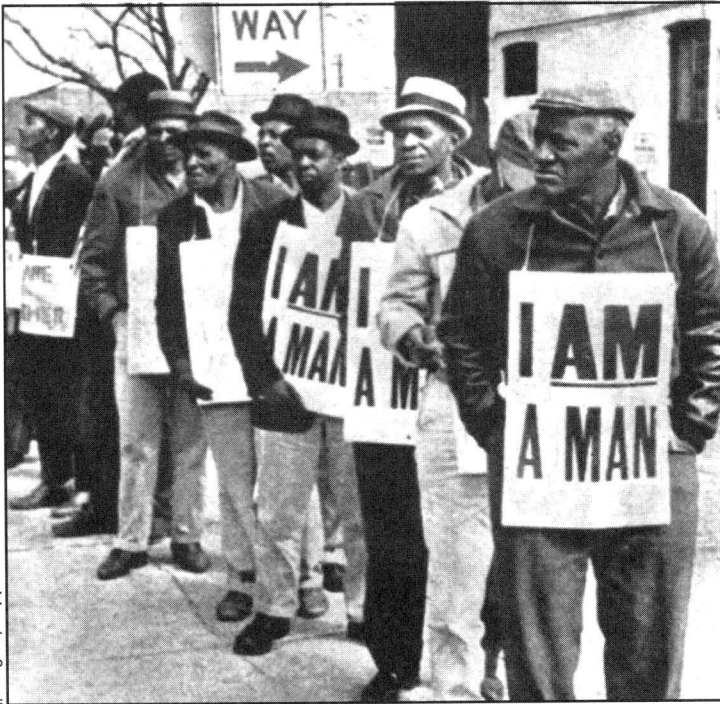

Maurice Sorrell

*The Memphis sanitation workers' strike of 1968 gained support from longshore workers and some southern white unionists, raising the potential for the "vast rallying of all the oppressed" predicted by Daniel Guérin.*

beginning, so long postponed, of a vast rallying of all the oppressed, set up as an independent political force...

...Such a rallying would undoubtedly give an impulse toward drawing the two races together, not only on the labor level, but in all social life. And since, on the other hand, it would encounter fierce resistance from the coalition of Northern and Southern business interests, it would have to engage in a struggle which might bring about a tremendous forward leap, not only for the

Negro race; but for all of American democracy.[83]

But the party theoreticians clung to their earliest formulations, despite the 1948 "Johnson" resolution. Party leader Cannon, however, tried to sidestep the issue and never spoke formally about his position in the dispute. He had moved to Los Angeles in the early '50s and no longer served on the Political Committee (the members of the National Committee residing in New York City). He never agreed with the nationalist line and supported Swabeck in his early talks with Trotsky. But Cannon feared a bitter faction fight on the issue.

Nevertheless, Cannon remained faithful to his original opposition to nationalism as the goal of the Black struggle. He believed strongly in the dual character of Black oppression—distinct from, yet integrally connected to, class struggle. Cannon wrote:

An honest workers' party of the new generation will recognize this revolutionary potential of the Negro struggle, and call for a fighting alliance of the Negro people and the labor movement in a common revolutionary struggle against the present social system...The movement of the Negro people and the movement of militant labor, united and coordinated by a revolutionary party, will solve the Negro problem in the only way it can be solved—by a social revolution.[84]

In 1953, the Revolutionary Integrationist minority outlined their ideas in a memorandum presented to the Political Committee, and held a public lecture series under SWP auspices in Los Angeles. The SWP leadership neither accepted nor challenged these ideas. The minority was, in effect, ignored. When Clara Fraser, a member of the Seattle SWP, attended the SWP's socialist education school in New

Jersey in 1953 and raised the question to George Breitman, he was virtually ignorant of the minority's thinking and sources, and rejected them without having studied any of the vast documentation on the subject.

The SWP was simply adapting to whatever *was* in the Black movement. And since Black workers and the community were aiming toward Revolutionary Integrationist goals in the '50s, no big disputes seemed imminent. Later, the line shifted in swift, dizzying, mind-boggling hopscotches as the movement's tactics and ideology changed rapidly during the civil rights battles of the '60s.

### 1957: A blessing on Rev. King

Every possible position was assumed by the party because of its "wait and see" policy. But it never waited very long before jumping to support any assertion of nationalism and reformism that erupted in the Black movement.

The 1957 convention resolution on the Black Question was enraptured with Dr. Martin Luther King, Jr.'s liberal pacifism. Instead of *critical* support, the leadership totally surrendered to King's religious, passive, establishment-oriented, and often irresponsible and dangerous leadership.

The 1963 Fraser resolution later explained:

> The SWP never acknowledges the crisis of leadership in the Black movement. The concept of "self-determination," a revolutionary demand when used by the Bolsheviks, is denuded of all meaning and becomes a rationale for the SWP position that anyone who is leading at the moment is a good leader and a destined leader, regardless of program. Since Negroes are a "nation," they are politically homogenous and united; an anatomy of the class divergence among them is accordingly academic, because it is not decisive for a

127

national movement. The important thing is to cement unity and not provoke dissension.[85]

Many theoreticians of the Black struggle, including Jean Simon of Los Angeles SWP and then Cleveland, were highly critical of the 1957 convention resolution. But like her, most of them, in time, were beaten down. They did not want to take on a headlong battle with George Breitman and the developing bureaucratic machine of Farrell Dobbs, Tom Kerry, and cohorts.

Most Blacks by now had left the party. A huge exodus occurred around 1950, due not only to the cold-war McCarthyite climate (the rationale proffered by the party regime), but to the genuine confusion of Black comrades in the face of a dual and contradictory party line.

Furthermore, the party's unconscious sexism worked to discourage and minimize the role of Black women. Clyde Cumming, a longtime theoretician, original member of the Revolutionary Integration minority, and a then-member of the Seattle Branch, was one of the few Black women activist leaders left in the party.

### Showdown at the 1963 convention

The supporters of Revolutionary Integration wrote a document that they introduced as a draft resolution for the 1963 SWP national convention.

The political climate in 1963 mandated the adoption of a clear policy for the party and the movement. The Black struggle had reached a dazzling new stage—it stood on the threshold of organizing for revolution. The movement sorely needed radical leadership, program, and direction to carry to conclusion the dismantling of the southern police state.

The party's course on the Black Question, by now mired in headaches and controversy, had to be altered. The majority resolution was titled "Freedom Now: The New Stage in the Struggle for Negro Emancipation and the Tasks of the SWP." It was written by George Breitman, and it shamelessly pledged all-out allegiance to nationalism—and to the already-discredited Black Muslims of Mr. Muhammad![86]

Clara Fraser was one of the main minority speakers in the incredibly heated debate. She took off on Breitman, Tom Kerry, and Robert Vernon, all strident nationalists.

> I pointed out the viciousness of Elijah Muhammad's position on Black women, his red-baiting virulence and anti-workingclass stance. I said that the SWP would be committing an irreparable error if it adopted the line of Elijah Muhammad for what was supposed to be a Bolshevik party.

> We had this knock-down...debate over nationalism vs. Revolutionary Integration, and the SWP voted its resolution up and down the line against the few votes we were able to muster. We were insulted and denigrated...by Tom Kerry.

> The official position of total support to Black nationalism was adopted at that convention, no question about it. Blacks are a nation by virtue of their culture, dialect, the ghetto, jazz and dancing and singing. Mr. Muhammad was a genius, and the Black movement was going to go to him.[87]

The regime's unprincipled and unprecedented vituperation against the minority vividly revealed the moral corruption, racism, and sexism of the Dobbs/Kerry bureaucracy. Instead of an illuminating debate of ideas, the regime resorted—and reverted—to the character assassination and demagogy expected at a Teamsters or Sailors convention, but not in the party of Leon Trotsky and James P. Cannon, who considered serious ideas from serious leaders very seriously!

It was hardly surprising to the minority when, shortly afterward, Malcolm X split from the Honorable Elijah Muhammad and the Black Muslims. Malcolm was moving leftward fast. Imagine the SWP's dismay and chagrin when Malcolm telegrammed George Lincoln Rockwell, head of the American Nazi Party: "This is to warn you that I am no longer held in check from fighting white supremacists by Elijah Muhammad's separatist Black Muslim movement...[and] that you and your Ku Klux Klan friends will be met with maximum physical retaliation."[88]

The SWP was so far behind the movement that only hopeless dogmatists could fail to see what had happened. Yet, in the next two years, this shameless bureaucracy drove the Revolutionary Integration minority—*and all other minorities*— from the party, and settled happily into monolithic sterility.

## SWP: The aftermath

The SWP today still waffles on the Black Question.

Its chronic refusal to take a scientific and class approach invariably ends in opportunist chasing after the rear echelons of the movement.

The 1963 resolution, "Freedom Now," had given uncritical support to the Black Muslims:

> [The SWP refutes] the slander that the Muslims and other separatists are "counterparts" of the White Citizens Councils and the Ku Klux Klan. It means counteracting the widespread but mistaken notion that separation, freely chosen by Negroes, is "equivalent" to segregation imposed by white supremacists.[89]

But did the SWP defend the nationalism of the Black Muslims by using the *Leninist criteria of nationhood and the right to self-determination?* No! They vulgarly supported nationalism under the guise and absolution that the Black Muslims wanted it.

The SWP's "A Transitional Program for Black Liberation" (1969) asks the way to Black liberation but never is able to answer the question.

Their program sets forth two tenets: that Blacks are an oppressed nationality (nation) *and* that Blacks are the most oppressed sector of the American working class:

> The hour has struck when an end must be put to all forms of exploitation and servitude. Full and definitive liberation cannot be achieved except through abolishing the private ownership of the means of production by the corporations and banks.

> This measure is mandatory whether Afro-Americans decide to exercise their right of self-determination through the creation of a separate black nation or within the context of the creation of a single socialist republic along with insurgent white workers and other anticapitalist forces.[90]

This "transitional program," as such, advocates the slogan of Black liberation through socialist revolution, but fails to delineate precisely *how* such a revolution is to occur. Are Blacks, despite their absorption into the American working class, supposed to believe that they can step aside and let white workers—filled with racism—dismantle the old system, and that this will usher in a new order of equity and justice for Blacks?

The SWP's ideology lacked simple logic and was a stranger to reality. It further gave the implicit prescription to Black comrades that only *they* could work in the Black movement; white comrades were supposed to sit on the sidelines and cheer them onward. And this was in 1969 when Blacks and white radicals were still working closely together on campuses, in the ghettoes, and in public actions.

Freedom Socialist Party forces, for instance, were *immersed* in Black community work. Most noticeably, the FSP was a public supporter and ally of the Black Panther Party and the Black Student Union on campus, and deeply involved with Blacks in the anti-poverty programs and mass community mobilizations for race justice.

The round of SWP resolutions dragged on until the 1975 resolution, "The Fight for Black Liberation," unwittingly exposed the bankruptcy of nationalism as a theory. The resolution extolled the exemplary role of the SWP during the civil rights movement of the 1960s, but mourned that "Despite the SWP's development of a program that could advance the Black movement, the Black revolutionary cadres were too few to make up for the leadership deficiencies that the Black struggle faced in the mid-1960s and early 1970s."[91]

Their program doesn't work, but who gets the blame? Black people, of course.

The 1975 resolution finally lets it all hang out:

"Centuries of oppression have welded Black people into a distinct nationality..."[92]

So now we know what it takes—centuries of oppression. But according to this definition, the Jewish people, or women, or gays, or Catholics suffering centuries of oppression are a nation. To the peculiar state of Israel, for example, we must now add a new Black "state."

This is an unscientific and irrational analysis. Centuries of oppression have caused the overwhelming majority of Blacks to long since opt for—self-determine—an integrationist struggle for full freedom and equality as citizens of the USA.

But the SWP jumps around eclectically, as always, indiscriminately supporting opponent tendencies and practices in the Black movement. Where Blacks are concerned, the SWP never sees class or political or religious or sex contradictions, just one happy monolithic nation.

The National Black Independent Party held its first national convention in Chicago in August 1981. Rightwing nationalists attempted to exclude all socialist organizations from membership. During the heated debate, the SWP remained silent. It had not a word of defense for itself or other representatives from the Left.

The SWP is becoming indistinguishable from the flabby social democrats and closet Stalinists in the mass movements. The wages of political sin are moral death.

# Revolutionary Integration in the turbulent 1960s

Black mass revolt at the height of the civil rights era— the '60s and early '70s—stunned the bourgeoisie, exposed and confronted its racist police state system, and made huge cracks in the pillars of racist capitalism.

But the movement was literally smashed at its height by the frenetic defense posture of the government. Hired gun for the bourgeoisie, the government killed, beat, and maimed scores of movement leaders and activists. Blacks were exiled, jailed, harassed, and intimidated en masse; Black churches were bombed by government-coddled provocateurs out to wreak havoc within and upon the movement.

A century had passed since the abolition of slavery. Yet as the world watched the televised evening news, a race of people was treated like a herd of cattle and rounded up for the slaughterhouse.

What the Democrats, Republicans, and FBI goons could

not liquidate, they attempted to buy off. The movement was further silenced by malicious government propaganda and rightwing ideology.

The retreat of the movement was caused by both objective and subjective phenomena. Its own internal weaknesses—lack of radical leadership and program—were magnified by its *lack of true allies.* Organized labor and white workers generally abstained from support, and the Left gave support, but played little of a vanguard political role. White radicals' cheerleading of Black nationalism, coupled with their treatment of *all* movements as mutually separate, operated to stall what might have been a vast united front.

### The Black reformists

Martin Luther King, Jr., symbol of the civil rights movement and Black reformism, was not a self-activated leader. His cry for human dignity and morality pricked the liberal consciousness. But actually, he was thrust forward by others—by Rosa Parks and Black *unionists* who sparked the Montgomery, Alabama bus boycott in 1955. As the respectable image of Blackness, a middleclass minister whom middle America could respect, he was a mass of contradictions. But when he turned toward Black labor—the Memphis garbage workers—his martyrdom was cast.

King was first and foremost a member of the Black pettybourgeoisie, and he possessed an unbreakable allegiance to the ruling class. He was their go-between with the movement.

The legacy he left to his people was the knowledge, which many already had, that Blacks had the power for unparalleled resistance and revolt.

As the movement gained confidence, it quickly bypassed King's pacifism, mysticism, and establishment ties. He was only one of the catalysts who helped create a spark which flamed into revolt.

His last days were his best. He was turning to Black

*Martin Luther King (at podium) and the community of Montgomery, Alabama vow to continue boycotting the segregated city buses in April 1956. An estimated 50,000 riders shunned the buses for 13 months in an action initiated by Black women of the Women's Political Council.*

workers, allying the civil rights struggle with organized labor and other social movements. His role in the Memphis, Tennessee garbage strike in 1968 and his denunciation of the Vietnam War were strong stands to take.

After King's assassination in Memphis in April 1968, his colleagues—the Jesse Jacksons, Ralph Abernathys, and Andrew Youngs[93]—took the helm of the civil rights movement and steered a clear course away from militancy. They led the mass reformist wing of the movement directly to the tutelage of the Oval Office.

Great reforms had been won—the Civil Rights Act and legislation of 1964, the Voting Rights Act of 1965, affirmative action programs, and more. But these gains, won by great travail, are becoming more and more precarious each day.

Reformist leaders and reformist demands are tenuous at best.

## The Black radicals

The Black movement has fostered scores of militant Black radicals whose courage, strength, tenacity, and ideas still inspire all movements for social justice throughout the world.

### Malcolm X

The great Black revolutionary leader Malcolm X, lived by his philosophy of "By Any Means Necessary." Malcolm's ascendancy to world prominence in the mid-'60s found the Black struggle at its zenith and sorely in need of his resolute boldness.

His scorn for the southern reformists found an answering echo in young and old southern militants, and galvanized the northern ghettoes.

Whether on street corners or podiums, Malcolm's fiery scorn ripped at the bastions of racism and spared no target. He was respected, emulated, admired, and feared. He was well on his way to becoming a great revolutionary and a Marxist. And he was gunned down on February 21, 1965 in New York City precisely at the moment when his split from the rabid nationalist and sexist Black Muslims was impelling him to an internationalist socialist perspective.

Malcolm and his followers were becoming a deadly serious threat to the ruling class. The Black Muslims and the FBI shot him dead to thwart that development. *They* have always used any means necessary.

### SNCC

The Student Non-Violent Coordinating Committee (SNCC) formed initially out of a conference called by Ella Baker, a Black civil rights veteran, for young members of the Southern Christian Leadership Conference (SCLC) in the spring of 1960 in Raleigh, North Carolina.

The youth of SCLC had grown up with the civil rights movement, beginning with the Montgomery bus boycott days in 1955. They had participated in scores of pacifist protests and demonstrations under Dr. King's leadership, and were growing more and more impatient at turning the other cheek. They had witnessed or were the victims of the barrage of violence unleashed on the movement by the southern police state.

Armed with the indomitable spirit of youth and angered by the frustrations, humiliations, and powerlessness of the movement, they wanted a new direction for struggle, different from the martyr syndrome, suffer-in-silence path of their parents and grandparents.

SNCC quickly veered away from the Christian moralism of SCLC and into militancy. Its leadership was composed of Black college-educated students, mostly male, and its membership grew with the addition of white college students, the majority of them women, who came to join them from the North, West, and South.

SNCC's delineation of an internal program was always in transition, beginning with the "Beloved Community" approach of SCLC, evolving into the "Let the People Decide" period and the thrilling "Black Power" interval, and then after other transitory phases, culminating in nationalism. But *externally* SNCC's purpose and direction were clear-cut.

SNCC had a "direct action" philosophy geared to topple the pillars of segregation—the Jim Crow laws. No more pleading with the southern crackers, no more tears.

SNCC carried out thorough organizing of the Black communities across the entire South and, to a limited extent, in the North. The organization worked arm-in-arm with the Black community and staged massive sit-ins, freedom rides, voter registration drives, and more. SNCC was a powerful organization whose fighting approach uplifted the civil rights movement; defeatism was replaced by defiance, and SNCC inspired, revived, or shamed the older generation into motion.

As a consequence, SNCC members were beaten, jailed, and murdered by the southern police and crackers, and harassed and framed by the FBI. But SNCC won proud and massive support from the Black community.

Early on, SNCC became fraught with the problems attendant to race, sex, and class. SNCC was a preview in microcosm of what would happen to the entire Black movement a few years later. SNCC was never able to resolve these conflicts, and the ensuing internal contradictions led to its demise.

*Women were the organizational driving force behind the administration of SNCC's day-to-day activities.* Without their skills and unremitting and courageous determination, the organization would never have gotten off the ground. The precise and efficient administration of the work flow was crucial to the success of SNCC's organizing activities, and women were relegated to these "secondary" posts, as well as to domestic duties in the Freedom Cooperative Houses.

SNCC women had to demand from the men the right to sit in or perform the more dangerous tasks that could provoke violence. This area of work had been reserved by the macho males as their own private property.

Black women contended for leadership within SNCC, and not too successfully. Yet they were at least as committed, aggressive, and bold as any male.

White women resented being relegated to support services, and they were surprised and disoriented and worried about the racial/sexual antagonisms caused by their whiteness. They had come to fight race prejudice and weren't prepared for prejudice against them. Many Black women, angered at the sexism of the males, became incensed at white women who had close relations with Black men. This broke down the promising feminist alliance between the Black and white women.

SNCC women presented a manifesto at a staff retreat in November 1964. It read in part:

> It needs to be known that just as Negroes were the crucial factor in the economy of the cotton South, so too in SNCC, women are the crucial factor that keeps the movement running on a day-to-day basis. Yet they are not given equal say-so when it comes to day-to-day decision-making. What can be done?[94]

Stokely Carmichael, then ascending to SNCC leadership, responded with his infamous and destructive answer: "The only position for women in SNCC is prone."[95]

Carmichael had bought right into the disgusting, super-sophisticated Moynihan Report, published in 1962. Daniel Moynihan, a Harvard sociology professor and later a Democratic politician, spewed forth the sexist and racist myth of the "Black matriarchy" and "the emasculating Black female." His long, clever book was written in scholarly style, and it exacerbated the growing division between Black men and women.

He blamed Black poverty and second-class citizenship on the "backward" Black family headed by a woman. Black men had to assert "manhood" and domestic control before they could be free. They had to be liberated from the matriarch.

Daniel Moynihan and the White House were out to skewer Black women leaders, and hence, the entire movement. Black male leaders dutifully condemned his book as distorted and dangerous, but the seed was planted. From that day onward, millions of Black men have sought to establish total personal, political, and emotional independence from Black women, and have blamed Black women for their "emasculation." Black women were made the enemy instead of white male capitalists.

Though SNCC members by then were more militant—influenced especially by Malcolm X's contempt for the reformist leaders in the South and for "whitey"—they were also growing demoralized. The sex/race conflict was driving out Black and white women alike. Southern justice was meting out more defeats and deaths.

Then Watts, the Black ghetto of Los Angeles, erupted in the summer of 1965 in a flame of revolt. SNCC was impressed. And in a final action, SNCC allied with the Mississippi Freedom Democratic Party (MFDP) at the Atlantic City, New Jersey convention of the Democratic Party in the summer of 1965. The goal was to seat an MFDP delegation to replace the all-white state machine.

Fannie Lou Hamer of the MFDP testified to the convention credentials committee that she had been denied the right to vote, had been jailed, and had been beaten. The following day at a rally she stated, "We are askin' the American people, 'Is this the land of the free and the home of the brave?'"[96]

The Democratic officials offered a compromise—they would seat the white delegation if it would take a loyalty oath and they would give delegate-at-large status to two MFDPers.

James Forman of SNCC commented: "Atlantic City was a powerful lesson, not only for the Black people from Mississippi, but for all of SNCC... No longer was there any hope...that the federal government would change the situation in the Deep South."[97]

In the summer of 1966, the slogan of "Black Power" suddenly emerged on a SNCC protest march in Mississippi. Stokely Carmichael took that slogan and popularized it through the national media. The rest is history. Carmichael became an entity unto himself, a public figure, a world personality who represented "Black Power."

Julius Lester, the Black writer, said in *Revolutionary Notes* that Carmichael became more than a representative of Black people:

> Slowly, the rhetoric and the aggressive image began to devour the Student Nonviolent Coordinating Committee and Carmichael. The rhetoric replaced program. The image replaced organizing. Sometimes it even seemed that Carmichael would say whatever was necessary to get the desired response, instead of saying whatever was necessary to build revolutionary consciousness.[98]

"Black Power" became one of the most ambiguous, misunderstood, and misused slogans of resistance of the decade. Its meaning was unclear to Black people and to white radicals. The white power structure thought for sure that all the forces of struggle were now united and the eve of revolution was at hand. But shortly after Carmichael's initial publicity blitz, white radicals were told to pack their bags, leave SNCC, and return to the white community, where Carmichael said they should do their organizing.

SNCC soon after declared itself to be a Black nationalist organization, and it slowly finished its degeneration.

A powerful, militant, and radical Black leadership organization had gone under, a victim of the race/sex and class contradictions that it could not—or would not—solve.

Clara Fraser in 1965, in an urgent exhortation to the SWP and to the Black movement, wrote:

> The Black liberation movement, North and South, to endure and develop, is going to have to rise to heights unachieved by any existing labor or political

organization: it is going to have to *come to grips with the woman question.*

White women will have to develop consciousness and militancy on this question and learn to bolster the course of Black women towards equality and leadership. Black women will have to see through the hypocrisy of the white middle-class norms of family stability and propriety. Black and white men will have to learn to subordinate subjective prejudices to a program and practice that incorporates appreciation of the woman question as an objective social issue that cannot be separated from civil rights. Equality and emancipation are indivisible...

...Black and white women, exerting their strength through solidarity, will soon persuade Black and white men to cease and desist from the habits and outlook of the slaveholder, and the movement will soar to new levels.[99]

## The Black Panther Party

The Black Panther Party formed as a direct result of police brutality in the ghettoes of the North and West. The crying need of the Black community was for self-defense.

The Panthers were greatly influenced by Malcolm X's revolutionary zeal and by his slogan, "By Any Means Necessary."

The Panthers organized "spontaneously." Two Blacks, Bobby Seale and Huey P. Newton, appeared on the scene in Oakland, California where police were arresting a Black person. They appeared with guns. It was 1966. And it made instant world headlines.

The Black Panther Party quickly became the open revolutionary, self-defense organization of the Black community. Its home was the ghetto and its purpose was the protection of Black people.

Panther history is a story of blazing courage, defiance against the system, and allegiance to the working class and poor of the Black community. Panther heroes, heroines, and revolutionary martyrs fill the pages of Black history and will long be remembered.

The very audacity of the party, however, proved to be its undoing. The Panther leadership was either brutally murdered or incarcerated as political prisoners, sorely weakening the party and frightening its ranks.

Their gun-toting image and mentality soon boomeranged. Their turn to lumpen elements as a priority for recruitment—in lieu of mass community organizing and

*The Black Panther Party's bold actions and revolutionary program grew out of the need for self-defense against police violence in the urban ghettos. Above, Huey Newton (with raised fist) speaks to a crowd of 7,000 in Philadelphia, PA in September 1970.*

waging an alliance with Black and white trade unionists—
prevented a mass-based membership. They looked for get-
rich-quick gimmicks, and there aren't any. They grew
desperate, and they disintegrated.

But during their brief existence, they were gloriously
anti-capitalist, internationalist, integrationist, and increasingly anti-sexist. Their demise is a tragic loss to the movement. One day, a more mature and less posturing party will
emerge to change the face of Black and white politics.

### Robert Williams: Blacks with guns

Armed self-defense as a basic survival tactic for besieged
Blacks actually came to the fore as an effective political strategy several years before formation of the Black Panther Party.

Monroe, North Carolina epitomized southern small-
town racism. Jim Crow laws had ghettoized the Black population into the neighboring community of Newton, and the
city for years had served as headquarters for the southeast-
ern network of the Ku Klux Klan, which operated in bra-
zen complicity with the local police.

And then the infamous "Kissing Case" emblazoned Monroe on the national and international map in 1957. Two Black
boys, ages seven and nine, were arrested and fraudulently
accused of "raping" a white girl. She had kissed one of the
boys on the cheek. Both boys were denied legal counsel and
sentenced to 14 years in prison after a "secret" trial.

Robert Williams, ex-Marine and a Black freedom activist, was forbidden to enter the courtroom when the verdict
was announced. He responded by mounting a national
defense campaign on behalf of the children. The case
achieved notoriety and Monroe authorities were forced to
acquit the pair and release them to their mothers.

Outraged at Monroe's mockery of civil rights, Williams
began to organize against the city's Jim Crow laws. Initially,
he tried to revive the defunct local NAACP.

Lacking support from Monroe's Black professional elite, Williams organized low-income and unemployed Blacks into a stunningly radical NAACP chapter. Supported by Black and white Freedom Riders, the chapter protested Monroe's segregated library and won a desegregated facility.

Williams then organized a picket of the public swimming pool where Blacks were banned from swimming with whites. A public protest was also mounted at the courthouse, atop of which the KKK normally displayed a lighted cross.

The Klan, in cahoots with other racists and the police, unleashed a reign of terror on Newton. Williams knew that relief by means of the legal system was impossible. So he fought fire with fire.

North Carolina law permitted gun ownership. Williams, a brilliant strategist, applied for and received a club charter from the National Rifle Association. The charter, unknown to the NRA, permitted the Black community to legally arm itself against the racist siege.

According to author Truman Nelson, Williams saw that:

> ...Negroes cannot receive justice from the courts. They must convict their attackers on the spot. They must meet violence with violence![100]

Williams coolly and systematically organized Newton into an armed camp, and the racist mobs bent on shooting, murdering, and pillaging the Black community were turned back. The armed Blacks of Newton bravely prevented full-scale genocide.

The later Black freedom fighters should have studied and absorbed William's defensive strategy, which was carefully measured to insure Black survival in the absence of legal remedies. Arming Blacks represented the revitalization of Black *revolt*; community self-defense is a revolutionary step for oppressed people with no other resources to

stave off terrorism.
Said Williams to Truman Nelson:

...I believe that when oppressed people show a will-
ingness to fight in formidable forces, the enemy, who is
a moral weakling and a coward, is more willing to grant
concessions and work for a respectable compromise.
Psychologically, we must also consider that the racist
whites consider themselves superior beings, therefore,
they are not willing to exchange their superior lives for
inferior ones. They are most vicious and violent when they
can practice violence with impunity.[101]

The final episode of Williams' struggle against the Monroe vigilantes is filled with irony.
Allegedly, a white couple wandered into Newton while
"sightseeing." They claimed to be unaware of the heated
racial climate between the Monroe and Newton communities, unaware that their lives were endangered by cross-
ing the border into the Black community.
Williams, fearing for their safety, harbored them in his
home, insuring their physical security amidst the racial
shooting war. Then he arranged their safe departure—and
found himself charged by local authorities and the FBI with
two counts of *kidnapping*!
He fled underground, becoming a hunted victim. He
was portrayed by the national media and the U.S. government as a "hardened, wanton, and armed criminal." He and
his family went to Cuba and lived there in exile for years.
They felt there was no safe haven anywhere within the racist borders of America. He visited China and Africa, and was
news wherever he went.
In 1962 while abroad, Williams recounted this incred-
ible tale of struggle and militant leadership, and elaborated
on the principle of armed self-defense in his book, *Negroes*

*with Guns.* Williams returned to the U.S. in 1969 and subsequently was acquitted of the charges against him and relieved of the tremendous weight of public slander and libel that had been leveled at him.

As of 1978, Williams was living in northern Michigan where he worked on an outreach program for the U.S.-China People's Friendship Association as well as doing community organizing and traveling around the country on the university lecture circuit.

### Impact of Blacks on labor

The labor movement's slogans are Solidarity... An injury to one is an injury to all... All for one, one for all.

But the American working class has always been divided along lines of race, caste, and sex. And these major divisions persist:

1. The separation between the aristocracy of labor and the labor bureaucrats on the one hand, and the rank and file on the other.

2. The division among relatively privileged workers and the superexploited workers—who are primarily people of color and women.

Trotsky stated to SWP leaders in 1939:

> The characteristic thing about the American workers' parties, trade-union organizations, and so on, was their aristocratic character. It is the basis of opportunism. The skilled workers who feel set in the capitalist society help the bourgeois class to hold the Negroes and the unskilled workers down to a very low scale. Our party is not safe from degeneration if it remains a place for intellectuals, semi-intellectuals, skilled workers...who build a very close milieu which is almost isolated from the genuine masses. Under these conditions our party cannot develop—it will degenerate.[102]

Not only will the party decay if it loses touch with the masses, so will labor. The labor movement itself cannot mature to class consciousness so long as it perpetuates racism, sexism, and control by its own aristocracy.

The racist backwardness of the U.S. labor movement is legendary, barring some notable exceptions. Delayed support to the Black struggle has greatly retarded both labor and the Black struggle.

Black workers historically have demanded an end to job segregation and discrimination; an end to Jim Crow union locals; equal job access; the right to unionize; equal wages, conditions, and seniority and, of late, super-seniority to prevent the "first fired" syndrome; labor solidarity against runaway shops and right-to-work laws; and support to civil rights struggles in the courts, legislatures, and on the streets. But Black workers have rarely received unstinting labor support.

During the height of the civil rights movement, the majority of white workers refused to see how their on-the-job struggle was tied directly to the fight of Blacks to achieve not only jobs and better working conditions, but full civil rights.

National labor recognition came to the civil rights movement only after great pressure and public exposure by Black and radical trade unionists, after pleas from and deals with the Black leadership, after widespread public sympathy for besieged Black workers in the South.

When the national merger of the AFL-CIO occurred in 1955, the new confederation announced a civil rights program to fight segregation and job discrimination in all its affiliated locals. In effect, this could have been a national constitutional ban against any union condoning on-the-job discrimination. However, what ensued were five long years of compromise, appeasement, and abstention of the AFL-CIO leadership from the issue.

There was no dismantling of segregation and discrimina-

*250,000 people of all races joined the March on Washington for Jobs and Freedom organized by African American unionists. It was the largest demonstration in U.S. history to that time.*

tion against Black workers, and no promised "organization drives."

## NALC/March on Washington

Disgusted Black unionists met in May 1960 and formed the Negro American Labor Council (NALC) in New York City.

NALC's membership was composed of union leaders and rank-and-filers. It was led by A. Philip Randolph, the only Black on the AFL-CIO executive board, and organizer-president of the Brotherhood of Sleeping Car Porters. NALC described itself as an autonomous body of Black trade unionists charged to work within the AFL-CIO to fight for and implement labor's original civil rights program.

NALC demanded an end to Jim Crow locals, to apprenticeship and training program freeze-outs, and to lockouts of Blacks by some unions. As A. Philip Randolph described it:

[The AFL-CIO] had accepted the fact that such solidarity was impossible to achieve in the South and proceeded "to perpetuate this racial division," even though it was clear that segregated unionism was the antithesis of effective trade-union organization. "Thus, they sowed the winds of the division of the workers upon the basis of race, and now they are reaping the whirlwinds."[103]

George Meany, arch-racist president of the AFL-CIO, publicly denounced Randolph and the NALC. He labeled them as a divisive group whose aim was to split and raise havoc with the AFL-CIO's all-out "advances" for racial equality.

NALC, undaunted, held its first convention in 1962 in New York City, where it developed plans for a "March on Washington" to demand jobs for Blacks and an end to industry and union bias. The march was scheduled for summer of 1963.

Martin Luther King, whose political vision had matured into a desire to unify the civil rights movement with struggling Black *workers,* contacted Randolph, encouraging him to expand the scope of the march to include pressure on Congress to enact the pending civil rights legislation which was being stymied by filibuster tactics.

NALC agreed to demand that freedom from race discrimination and on-the-job protections be included in the legislation—a multi-pronged attack.

*This* March on Washington happened, and it was the most successful labor demonstration of the century in the nation's capital. Two hundred thousand civil rights fighters and forty thousand trade unionists participated.

The AFL-CIO executive board condemned the march by a majority vote.

Then in 1964, the most comprehensive civil rights legislation ever enacted was passed by a frightened Congress. Included in the measure were voting rights, access to equal education, and fair employment practices. Title VII of the law prohibited unions and employers of more than 100 workers from discrimination in employment, membership, apprenticeship, and promotion of "any individual because of race, color, religion, sex, or national origin."

NALC and civil rights workers understood well the absolute necessity for labor's alliance with the civil rights struggle. NALC subsequently proceeded to help the civil rights movement secure labor support for voter registration drives throughout the South.

### Selma

In February 1965, war was declared on the voter registration drive organized by Martin Luther King, and the city of Selma, Alabama was drenched in terror.

To stop the drive, Klan-member Sheriff Jim Clark called in the National Guard. Two people were killed and hundreds jailed. Viola Liuzzo, a white activist and wife of a Detroit Teamster leader, was murdered.

In response, the Black community reached out to the nation and to organized labor, and welded together an astonishing unity of different forces. They all marched from Selma to Montgomery, Alabama to protest the terrorism and promote their cause.

After a protracted struggle, Sheriff Clark and the city government conceded. The united front policy of the civil rights workers had won.

In July 1965, Congress passed the Voting Rights Act, finally granting *in law* the right of Black men and women to vote.

This legislation had hardly been enacted when Watts, Los Angeles' Black ghetto, exploded.

### Watts

August 1965. White America is stunned. Why did Blacks turn to utter destruction of their own community when they had received so much?

The Black petty-bourgeoisie, distant and guilt ridden, questioned in a similar vein. But the Black working class, radicals, and a few liberals knew why Watts went up in smoke.

All the legislative enactments and promises by labor did not dissipate the gross poverty, lessen unemployment, or alleviate repression in northern and western ghettoes.

Jobs might have helped to prevent the explosion, but the issue was broader than simple employment. Blacks who had jobs were in menial, marginal, service/trade, "Black" jobs. And even those with better jobs were still largely unorganized. If Blacks were unionized, they generally needed better wages, a chance for upward mobility, affirmative action compliance, and participation in the union leadership.

Following Watts, Martin Luther King urged a joint struggle by organized labor and the civil rights movement to open a new road for the whole nation, a road that would lead to those immediate gains not encompassed in the civil rights "victories"—*jobs* and *union organizing*.

In the summer of 1967, the ghettoes in Detroit, Newark, and Cleveland also went up in flames. Black fury was at fever pitch.

## Memphis sanitation strike

In Memphis, Tennessee, Black sanitation workers turned the union-busting city government upside down. Starting in February 1968, 1,200 members of AFSCME Local 1773 had staged a 65-day, nationally publicized strike for wage increases and safe working conditions.

Memphis had been previously untouched by civil rights agitation. Mayor Loeb, a racist tyrant, instituted terrorism against the striking workers.

King and national labor responded to the pleas of the workers and the civil rights movement. Special support came from the International Longshoremen's and Ware-housemen's Union (ILWU). And then, King, who was in Memphis to help, was assassinated by a sniper's bullet on April 4, 1968.

The Black/labor alliance had been truly underway, which is why King was gunned down. A few days later, the strike was won. But the movement receded from that point on.

## Charleston hospital strike

Charleston, South Carolina had been bypassed by both the CIO organizing drives of the 1930s and the civil rights movement—to its obvious detriment. Charleston was the home of J.P. Stevens Co., the giant runaway-shop enterprise which controlled Charleston with an iron fist. The company owned 23 textile mills throughout South Carolina.

In March 1969, the service workers of two county and city hospitals went out on strike for union recognition, wage increases, and a grievance procedure. The strikers were affiliated with Local 1199B of the Drug and Hospital Workers Union.

The majority of the strikers were Black women and their leaders were Black women.

The entire workingclass Black community supported the strike with massive boycotts of white businesses, demonstrations, and picket lines.

Governor McNair vowed that the state would never recognize a public employee union. Mass arrests were made and the National Guard turned the city into an armed camp.

Nationally, the strike received support from the AFL-CIO, and the ILWU threatened to shut down Charleston's port.

In July 1969, the hospital workers won their four-month-long struggle. After the victory, Coretta Scott King, widow of the slain civil rights leader and a strong supporter of Local 1199B, stated that the alliance A. Philip Randolph had devoted a lifetime to building—"the alliance of civil rights groups and organized labor—is a reality today in Charleston."[104]

Apart from the tremendous strike support by the Black community, what impressed her most about the struggles, she declared, was "the emergence of Black women leaders as a new breed of union leaders." She was referring to women like Mary Ann Maultree, the leader of Local 1199B, "They will be a source of great pride to the Black people and to the entire labor movement."[105]

However, both in Memphis and Charleston, only limited support had been forthcoming from *southern* workers.

## The League of Revolutionary Black Workers

A significant development in northern labor, shortly before the Black movement receded, was the formation of Black militant caucuses in Detroit's auto plants. The caucuses, many of which were called RUM (Revolutionary Union Movement), had formed in response to the entrenched racism of the United Auto Workers (UAW) leadership. This union had once been in the forefront of the civil rights struggle.

Dodge RUM (DRUM), Eldon Avenue RUM (ELRUM), and other autonomous caucuses merged into the League of Revolutionary Black Workers (LRBW) in 1969.[106]

The league demanded equal pay for equal work, an end to the prevalent seniority system which favored "first hired" white workers, full Black representation in leadership of the UAW, and implementation of the affirmative action guidelines enunciated in the Civil Rights Act of 1964.

The tactics of the league were to call unauthorized shutdowns of the plants for differing periods of time until grievances were remedied. But the league's mistake was to separate itself from white workers who supported its demands. The ultra-leftism and isolation of the wildcat strikes quickly brought about the league's downfall.

Though the League of Revolutionary Black Workers was the vanguard force of radical Black labor in the late '60s, its internal conflicts over Black nationalism tore the organization to pieces and a number of splits resulted. The LRBW executive was also openly hostile to women's liberation, and like its successor, the Black Workers Congress, never developed a concrete program for dealing with the special problems facing women in the auto plants.

By late 1971, LRBW had faded into history.

## *Twilight*

In the late 1960s, a general mood of despair hovered over the civil rights movement. Although the reformists would not admit it, the time for reforms was over. The revolutionaries were dead or dropouts or co-opted, and many militants drifted away or capitulated to what they called nationalism, but was in essence *cultural nationalism*. Cultural nationalism is classless, superficial, conservative, and antipolitical, without an ounce of revolutionary potential.

Slowly but noticeably, the Black community went back home. Tired and demoralized, it closed the door on mass action.

June Jordan, in "Poem on the Murder of Two Human Being Black Men," memorializes two Black students from Southern University who were killed during campus unrest, and she pinpoints the dominant mood:

> ...I'm tired
> and you're tired
> and everybody's goddamn tired
> tired
> students tired
> Blackfolks tired
> Liberals tired
> Revolutionaries tired...[107]

# The 1970s: Cultural nationalism and Black macho

The militancy of the 1960s and early 1970s recoiled. The radical leaders were crushed and the scene was set for the rightwing cultural nationalists to take center-stage.

Historically, Black nationalism becomes a dominant force within the Black struggle *only after all other avenues of resistance have been crushed.* And contemporary cultural nationalism represents resigned adaptation to the fascism of forced segregation. It is, moreover, the consummation of an opportunist strategy.

Stokely Carmichael and Black political scientist Charles V. Hamilton wrote in *Black Power:*

> [Black Power] is a call for black people in this country to unite, to recognize their heritage, to build a sense of community. It is a call for black people to begin to define their goals, to lead their own organizations and to support those organizations. It is a call to reject the racist institutions and values of this society. The concept...rests on a fundamental premise: *Before a group can enter the open society, it must first close ranks.* By this we mean that group solidarity is necessary before a group can operate effectively from a bargaining position of strength in a pluralistic society.[108]

The authors here define the right and necessity of oppressed groups to function autonomously *for a period* in order to accomplish their goals. But a little more Marxist application, clarification, and precision are needed to clarify this tactic.

Autonomy as a tactic must flow from the specific situation of the oppressed group. The situation must *warrant* the temporary application of autonomy.

Autonomy, however, never means *abstention* from class

struggle. Ideally, it coincides with and engenders heavy in-volvement in class struggle.

The tactic of autonomy becomes dangerous when it is raised to the level of a political principle, i.e., "Cultural Autonomy," or separatism. It is a fatal misapplication of the "Black Power" slogan.

Black militants took this audacious slogan, which never originally dealt with nationhood, and made it into a nation-alist slogan implying a call for a separate state. "Black Power" was transformed from a tactic into a matter of program, and its application became an excuse for abstention from and disinterest in class struggle. As Megan Cornish explains:

> Cultural separatism considers its entire culture, *in-cluding its own ruling class,* as superior to all others. This entrenches the domination over the workers by "their own" bourgeoisie and sets them against their real allies, the workers of other nations. The cultural sepa-ratists inevitably fail to challenge imperialism... Its in-capacitating effects are evident in sectors of all democratic movements. People are deflected away from struggle against the enemy; they become divisive and try to destroy the left wing and the militants.[109]

The first time that "Black Power" and "Black Pride" rang out at a SNCC protest march in 1965, they were a celebration of group solidarity and group impact, a re-joicing in the strength of Blackness, so long denied to, and by, Blacks. Black Pride meant cultural recognition of the beauty of Blackness, and Black Power meant the goal of political power—a rejection of powerlessness. Negroes were now Black people by their own definition, no longer "niggers."

Then Carmichael turned into a nationalist, and the na-tionalists applied the slogans to *separatism.* The highly posi-

Faith Ringgold

*In* Black Macho and the Myth of the Superwoman, *Michele Wallace broke every taboo, fearlessly examining relations between African American women and men, white racism, internalized oppression, homophobia and more.*

tive elements of these cries turned into what the Panthers aptly called "pork-chop" nationalism, a cultural nationalism shorn of class struggle, internationalism, and socialism.

Since this rhythm-and-soul nationalism lacked any proletarian analysis of society, it could offer no program for resistance, no viable goals or demands. But Black males loved it—those males who had wholeheartedly adopted bourgeois sexism and Professor Moynihan's garbled theory of the emasculating Black female.

Black males went on to glorify, indeed to deify, the BLACK MAN, the BROTHERS, the almighty BLACK BROTHER, and MANHOOD. Soon, the sheer amount of super-macho strutting around attained the level of the absurd.

But afros and dashikis and medallions did not a rebel make. The capitalists had created malleable male peacocks and aspiring middleclass executives; the divide-and-conquer tactics of male supremacy and nationalism had worked like charms against the Black movement.

Black women had already left the movement in droves because of the virulent sexism. And they took with them all the drive and impetus that had fueled the movement.

In "Reflections on the Black Woman's Role in the Community of Slaves," Angela Davis stated:

> The status of women in any given society is a barometer measuring the overall level of social development... As Franz Fanon has masterfully shown, the strength and efficacy of...revolutionary movements bear an immediate relationship to the range and quality of female participation.[110]

Clara Fraser had already said it in *Crisis and Leadership* in 1965. This was the giant issue that characterized the '70s Black movement—the battle of the sexes.

On the surface, the movement had a limited bread-and-butter program for elementary demands. But this period was also delineated by intense introspection and exploration of the future course of the struggle. The most intense and important debate occurred between Black women and men on the role of women.

Here is how male and female roles were defined in a Black nationalist pamphlet in the early '70s:

> We understand that it is and has been traditional that the man is the head of the house/nation because his knowledge of the world is broader, his awareness greater, his understanding is fuller and his application of this information is wiser... After all, it is only reasonable that

the man be the head of the house because he is able to defend and protect the development of his home... Women cannot do the same things as men—they are made by nature to function differently. Equality of men and women is something that cannot happen even in the abstract world. Men are not equal to other men, i.e., ability, experience, or even understanding. The value of men and women can be seen as in the value of gold and silver—they are not equal but both have a great value. We must realize that men and women are a complement to each other because there is no house/ family without a man and his wife. Both are essential to the development of any life.[111]

What a stupid resurrection of the treacherous ideology of "Kinder, Kirche, Küche" of the Third Reich![112]

The contradiction between the blatant sexism of Black men, especially the nationalists, and the growing feminist consciousness of Black women, led the sisters to publicly dissociate themselves from the third-class, "nigger" status that the brothers so graciously assigned them. Black women, traditionally independent and self-reliant, were instinctive or conscious feminists, and they took to the books to retrace their real historic role as Black women and to refute the slanders of the men.

Many stood up to the brothers. Others broke or became confused under the hammer-blows. One of the great problems they faced was the current of racism and rampant careerism glaringly evident in the new women's movement. Nevertheless, early cooperation between white and Black feminists was marked and enthusiastic.

Black women were among the first to raise feminism by means of militant struggle, especially in the fight for abortion. Black women in general found it difficult to completely separate race from class and sex oppression; they experienced all forms of harassment simultaneously and understood the interconnections.

As Beverly Smith, a Black lesbian feminist, stated:

> ...I feel it is radical to be dealing with race and sex and class and sexual identity all at one time. I think *that* is really radical because it has never been done before...

> ...we are not one dimensional, one-issued in our political understanding. Just by virtue of our identities we certainly define race and usually define class as being fundamental issues that we have to address...[113]

## Rebirth and retreat of Black feminism

As most Black men were drifting away from the struggle in the '70s, Black women were the soul-survivors and inheritors of the struggle. They were searching for a theory, program, and radical course of action that would weld their feminism to their struggle as Blacks.

They demanded to fight as *whole women* against all the enemies they faced:

> Black women have always embodied, if only in their physical manifestation, an adversary stance to white male rule and have actively resisted its inroads upon them and their communities in both dramatic and subtle ways. There have always been Black women activists—some known, like Sojourner Truth, Harriet Tubman, Frances E.W. Harper, Ida B. Wells Barnett and Mary Church Terrell, and thousands upon thousands unknown—who had a shared awareness of how their sexual identity combined with their racial identity to make their whole life situation and the focus of their political struggles unique. Contemporary Black femi-

nism is the outgrowth of countless generations of political sacrifice, militancy and work by our mothers and
sisters.[114]

And what was the reaction of the brothers, those super-
revolutionaries, to this gut-level manifesto from their doubly oppressed sisters?

There were a few men who did not want to lose their
female allies and comrades. They listened, absorbed,
sought to understand, and worked to change. Others refused to stop their arrogant, humiliating, demeaning, and
superior-elitist ways of interacting with Black women. For
the most part, Black women's pleas fell on deaf ears, fatally
inflated egos, and an already dead consciousness.

### The isolation of Black feminists

Michele Wallace, a Black writer, cracked the whole question of Black sexism wide open in her 1979 book *Black Macho and the Myth of the Superwoman*. Wallace's stunning
contribution to Black theory came from her commitment to
tell the truth—regardless of who didn't want to hear it.

Her book is an uncompromising and candid portrayal
of Black machismo stripped bare, and it raised the ire of
many Black males; you did not have to be a radical to catch
the message. Her thesis reached into the Black community
and jolted millions of nerve endings.

Wallace, however, was caught in a dilemma, like other
Black women who had awakened to feminism. As an out-
front feminist, the isolation she experienced from the Black
community, coupled with her estrangement from most
white middleclass feminists, led her to state in "A Black
Feminist's Search for Sisterhood":

But for now, Black feminists, of necessity it seems,
exist as individuals—some well known, like Eleanor

Holmes Norton, Florynce Kennedy, Faith Ringgold, Shirley Chisholm, Alice Walker, and some unknown, like me. We exist as women who are Black and who are feminists, each stranded for the moment, working independently because there is not yet an environment in this society remotely congenial to our struggle—because, being on the bottom, we would have to do what no one else has done; we would have to fight the world.[115]

Fighting the world is a big order, yet the plunge into feminism forced many Black women to this political crossroads in the '70s. Which will it be for us, they asked, an interracial women's movement or a separate, autonomous Black women's movement?

The feminism of middleclass white women had never held much appeal for Black women, nor had bourgeois feminists extended much of a welcome to them. Socialist feminism was hardly a mass movement. And an independent Black women's movement would elicit Black male rage.

As Audre Lorde wrote in "Who Said It Was Simple":

> But I who am bound by my mirror
> as well as my bed
> see causes in color
> as well as sex
>
> and sit here wondering
> which me will survive
> all these liberations [116]

What happened to the grand new interracial alliance of Black and white feminists? It was ferociously attacked by Black males and their Black women ideological captives who spouted nationalism with a vengeance bred of hatred for the white-woman-competitor. It was attacked by racist white feminists and by white socialists who were cheerleaders for Black nationalists. And it was attacked by the bosses, who are always quick to spot trouble.

Black feminists suffered terrible threats and harassment and insults from all sides. Black macho nationalism went on to devastate the Black movement and to wreak havoc on the women's movement. Shorn of the leadership and drive of Black women, both movements reeled, and neither has yet recovered.

But recovery is in sight. The simple truth is that feminism cannot exist in racial isolation or in a political vacuum, severed from a radical program and structure and oblivious to race and class struggles. As on-the-job struggles increase, Black and white women are gaining valuable experiences in cooperation. These new relationships carry over into collaboration on race and sex and sexuality issues outside the workplace as well.

Feminism, moreover, is concrete and alive only when its goal is to build a new socialist society based on complete freedom and on material, emotional, intellectual, and political fulfillment. And the same is true for anti-racism; it demands a revolutionary perspective and grasp if it is to grow and broaden. The Black woman will soon find the "simple" answer in common work with other women of color and with her white socialist sisters.

The mass movement is where the marriage of feminism and radicalism first takes place. And movement experience prepares the most advanced and capable sisters of color for political union with a welcoming, egalitarian, and disciplined socialist feminist collective that appreciates and respects their leadership.

The "me" who survives "all these liberations" will be the total and indivisible socialist feminist warrior. Black feminism can only survive in the context of revolutionary politics, unlike white feminism whose largest sector is middleclass, careerist, upwardly mobile, and pro-Establishment. Among Black women, there aren't enough of this reformist type to sustain such a movement, especially in the face of Black male and white racist hostility.

Any organization that fights seriously for race and sex equality and for workers' rights might just as well go socialist in the bargain, given the calumny sure to be heaped on its head! When reformism dies, the only "philosophically active" pro-feminist and pro-Black liberation ideology is revolutionary Marxism.

## Socialist feminism

The Freedom Socialist Party and Radical Women were the first, and remain the only, revolutionary organizations to present a realistic socialist feminist answer to Black women—a radical, disciplined, and all-encompassing solution to the problems of race, sex, sexuality, and class struggle.

A program that is itself rooted in the Black movement, socialist feminism lives in the battles of all people of color, in the lesbian/gay movement, in the class struggle.

Revolutionary feminism also happens to be an integral part, a cornerstone, of every movement. It objectively answers the ideological search of Black women and men. It is the political foundation of the new revolutionary vanguard: *socialist feminist people of color.*

A number of Black women pioneers became socialist feminists in the mid-'60s and '70s, and they had an enormous impact on every struggle they joined. At first they felt comfortable with their white comrades. But inevitably the cultural nationalist pressures from Black conservatives—and from nationalist radicals—plunged them into inner conflict. The toughest hung tough, of course; the others capitulated or retreated.

Yet new Black faces steadily turn up in the socialist feminist sector as Black women pursue their quest for a program, a style of action, and a commitment that makes sense.

## Black lesbians and gay men

Lorraine Hansberry, the young, gifted, and Black prophet, wrote in 1957 to a lesbian periodical, *The Ladder:*

> I think it is about time that equipped women began to take on some of the ethical questions which a male dominated culture has produced and dissect and analyze them quite to pieces in a serious fashion. It is time that "half of the human race" had something to say about the nature of its existence. Otherwise—without revised basic thinking—the woman intellectual is likely to find herself trying to draw conclusions—moral conclusions—based on acceptance of a social moral superstructure which has never admitted to the equality of women and is therefore immoral itself. As per marriage, as per sexual practices, as per the rearing of children, etc. In this kind of work there may be women to emerge who will be able to formulate a new and possible concept that homosexual persecution and condemnation has at its roots not only social ignorance, but a philosophically active anti-feminist dogma...[117]

Lorraine Hansberry's vision was an accurate forecast of things to come. Twenty-two years later, in 1979, Third World lesbians and gays stood up and let it be known once and for all that "We ain't gonna take it, not gonna take it anymore."

The first National Third World Lesbian/Gay Conference was held in Washington, D.C. in October of that year, in conjunction with the National Lesbian/Gay March on the nation's capital which brought together an estimated quarter of a million lesbians and gays of all colors to demand sexual and racial freedom.

*The Third World Contingent at the 1979 National Lesbian/ Gay March on Washington brought together workingclass African American lesbians and gays, radically challenging homophobia, racism and sexism in every community.*

The conference, organized by the National Coalition of Black Gays, signaled the end of the '70s, the rejection of President Jimmy Carter's hypocritical, paternalistic, heaven-centered platitudes; the end of age-old subjugation of Third World lesbians and gays by their communities.

This conference and march changed the course of the people of color movements by throwing off the shackles of invisibility and openly asserting Third World lesbian/gay leadership in the beleaguered race, sex, sexuality, and workingclass movements.

This was a milestone for Third World struggles—a defiant, militant, international challenge by those on the bottom of the bottom, now rising and stating their minds. Claudia Hinojosa and Max Mejia, members of the Mexican lesbian/gay Lambda and also of Mexico's Trotskyist party, the PRT (Partido Revolucionario de los Trabajadores), read a statement to the conference:

> Our struggle consists of the subversion of all concepts and practices which have defamed lesbians and gay men, and subjugated women in general. The struggle against sexism, racism, imperialism, and class oppression is integral to gay liberation. We wish to leave no aspect of daily life unchallenged.[118]

Before joining the March on Washington, the Third World Contingent, which included the Freedom Socialist Party and Radical Women, marched from the conference site through the Black and Asian American communities of the capital. FSP and RW's billowing banner proudly displayed the slogan: "Lesbian/Gay Liberation Through Revolutionary Socialist Feminism."

How similar, yet different, that march was compared to Black protests through the years in Washington, D.C.— demonstrations by early suffragists which included Black women; A. Philip Randolph and the huge 1964 march on Washington by Black labor and civil rights activists; the civil rights mobilizations and the Poor People's March. *Things had changed, something new had been added; for once, all the closets were open.* The general movements for social change now meshed and intersected, with Third World lesbians and gays dancing in the streets.

It was a great beginning. Sexual bigotry has at last come to the fore as an issue to be dealt with, explained, and excoriated. And this is happening none too soon; sexism and homophobia run rampant in the Black community.

Consider the way the government used homophobia to deflect the hunt for possible white racists behind the child murders in Atlanta, Georgia in 1979-1981. Wayne Williams, a Black man, was accused of being a homosexual and the prosecutors insinuated that his sexuality lay behind the slaughter of Atlanta's Black children. The government's approach assured that Williams would *not receive broad community support,* and the furor aroused against him served to hide the prosecution's incredibly weak case.

Twenty-nine young people were killed, mostly boys. And a Black man was found who could be blamed. He could be *safely* blamed because the magic word "homosexuality" had been whispered and good old divide-and-conquer did the rest.

Further, the media outcry about the dead children masked the ongoing slaughter of *women* in that city. An editorial in Boston's *Gay Community News,* "Atlanta Vertigo: A Dispatch from the Front," pointed out:

> While we have been inundated with reports of missing and murdered Black boys and men, no screaming headlines have publicized the grotesque number of Womyn murdered here. Not a week goes by without some Woman's body turning up on a back page of the paper... In fact, femicide is the leading cause of death for Black Womyn, ages 20-30, according to police statistics.
>
> But that's *normal,* after all. Womyn just get killed; and mostly it's the old man doing it. No one wants to examine things too closely here...[119]

The divide-and-conquer danger faced most urgently by lesbians and gays of color was addressed by Black poet Pat Parker in her 1978 poem, "Where Will You Be?":

> ...It won't matter
> if you're

Butch, or Fem
Not into roles
Monogamous
Non
Monogamous

It won't matter
If you're
    Catholic
    Baptist
    Atheist
    Jewish
    or M.C.C.

They will come
They will come
to the cities
and to the land
to your front rooms
and in *your* closets.

They will come for
the perverts
and where will
you be
When they
come?[120]


Parker's message is plain: unity is a survival necessity. That is why the Third World lesbian/gay movement is an abiding hope for all the social movements.

It is a bold challenge to the blatant sexism and homophobia suffusing the people of color movements, and it is also the vehicle for tackling the intra-group racism of Third World communities. Here, the super-oppressed of all colors are banded together against a common oppression that cuts through color divisions.

The most urgent task facing this new movement is to realize its revolutionary potential by ridding itself of its nationalist tendencies and shaking off its ties with reformism.

This task can be accomplished. And the program of the Freedom Socialist Party is the vehicle for its success. It offers a theoretical and concrete antidote to the poison of divide-and-conquer tactics that have wracked the social movements for so long.

The Third World lesbian/gay movement must take a militant stand and weld together the ranks of a truly unified mass movement—a united front integrated on all levels—that will be more than ready for the day when "they" come!

### The road ahead

The Black feminism that resurfaced in the dynamic '60s, receded in the gathering gloom of the '70s.

Nonetheless, despite all the contradictions that beset them, the most courageous women and men *did* find a synthesis: socialist feminism. Today, these revolutionaries battle the interlinked realities of race, sex, and class oppression and demand the rightful equality of women leaders within every movement—in labor, in the arts and literature, in the race and sex struggles.

Black woman radicals are bravely opening doors not only for the Black struggle, but for all movements for progressive social change. The implications have been, and are, far-reaching.

Revolutionary feminists of all colors, working together, create a bond which keeps movements alive, which breathes new life into them and carries them forward.

And hearken to the dialectics of the sexual revolution: the vitality of the Black lesbian/gay sector is the catalyst for restoring the entire Black movement to the revolutionary path!

# The 1980s: The Black movement in the Reagan era

The rightward political shift which unleashed the power and viciousness of the reactionaries at the beginning of this decade has thrust a huge sector of labor and a significant proportion of Blacks toward militancy and the Left.

Blacks and labor can no longer surrender to easy cynicism, despair, and disgust. Nor can they adopt the prevailing and rampant petty-bourgeois narcissistic self-absorption. The escalation of the diabolical Reaganesque reaction forces the poor to sell out, starve—or fight back. The opportunity has never been better to seize the time and build a vital, massive united front.

Reagan's regime has accelerated the steady deterioration of social programs since the '60s and imposed a reign of social terror to go with its economic blitzkrieg. The Black community, as in all periods of economic bust and political reaction, is facing a frontal assault.

## *Misery and terror for the Black community*

At this writing, the official national unemployment rate for Black adults is over 20%—and a staggering 52% for Black teenagers! Reagan's program of "balancing the budget" on the backs of Blacks and the poor includes the plan to demolish the Voting Rights Act, affirmative action guidelines, any remaining social services, and abortion/reproductive rights.

This Hollywood front man for Wall Street has slashed $2.5 billion in welfare allotments and social services, plus 300,000 public service jobs under the federal CETA (Comprehensive Education and Training Act) program, and he has plans for further cuts. The denial of abortion to poor women forces many Black women to give birth to children they cannot feed, clothe, or house.

Reagan's opposition to busing, his proposed tax exemptions for private racist educational institutions, and his "new federalism" plan are sideshow hustles accompanying the main act—smashing unions, lowering wages, and further robbing workers and the poor.

The ruling class can only succeed in its increased rate of theft from the people by preventing *new waves of militant protest* from rising up from the bottom layer of society, from the disenchanted surplus labor force.

The ruling class directs Reagan to increase his genocidal programs against Blacks in order to make certain that Blacks are too busy trying to stay alive to fight back.

## The Black struggle and the Left

Most radical organizations are concerned with and give a high priority to their involvement in the Black struggle, especially given the new stirrings caused by Reaganomics.

Black community coalitions and ad hoc groups abound on vital issues like the Ku Klux Klan, police brutality, and civil rights. These groups are important vehicles for fighting the right wing, building radical alliances, and laying the groundwork for the emergence of united fronts.

But work in the Black community must be carefully and constantly evaluated, and handled with the utmost care. Established or promising alliances are always tentative and easily broken. Effective community organizing stems from correct theory, realistic program, and tactical good sense, all of which flow from a left group's position on the Black Question.

And these positions are in wide disarray today.

### CP adaptation and opportunism

The U.S. Communist Party adapts not only to current moods of the Black movement, but to capitalism itself. The road to Black liberation, according to the CP, is through the Democratic Party machine.

CP luminary and mentor and distinguished academic,

Angela Davis, attempts in her 1981 book, *Women, Race and Class,* to integrally connect sex oppression to race oppression and class struggle. But she fails to achieve her goal. Davis lends mere lip service to feminism and offers only grudging and inconsistent support to lesbian/gay rights. Her deliberate omission of Black lesbianism in the movement, and her refusal to challenge rampant Black male sexism, exposes her party's theoretically frail position on the Woman Question.

Regardless of the CP's social-democratic, demagogic, and opportunist *claim* of support to feminism, Davis and the CP maintain that sexism is a minor issue in comparison to the entrenched racism of this society. The progressive movements must deal with racism first, she says; other forms of oppression are real, but are only a secondary nuisance under capitalism.

Davis and the CP are wildly incorrect. Sexism and homophobia appeared in history *prior* to racism. Sexism was the *model* for racism, not vice versa. Also, Black sexism paralyzes the battle against racism. As a matter of fact, sexism has seriously eroded the impact of Angela Davis both as a Black leader and as a Communist, though she pretends not to notice!

Davis' public affiliation with communism is brave and independent. But the program she represents is little more than old-fashioned, ultra-conservative *nationalism.* Davis is a superstar as an historian, philosopher, activist, and personality, but as a theoretician of Blackness she has little sound advice for Black women or Black men—or white radicals.

The CP line ends up as a distinct disservice to its Black proponents, to the Black struggle, and to socialism.

## The Trend

The Trend, an opportunist Stalinist configuration associated with the journal *Line of March,* maintains that

U.S. Blacks do not comprise a nation but are a key sector within the U.S. working class.

The Trend says that racism is the "primary contradiction" in U.S. society and carries this line to its programmatic extreme, implying that the race question is more important than, and supersedes, the class struggle as a whole.

The Trend sells out and maligns feminism and lesbian/gay liberation and refuses to acknowledge the connection of these struggles to the movement against racism. The Trend is blind to the fact that all the liberation movements are interlinked, and that their *combination* will propel the U.S. working class forward.

The Trend redbaits grassroots and radical leaders in the movements, and orients almost exclusively toward liberals and pacifists, blurring class lines in order to win popularity with them.

According to the Trend, the masses tend to follow only conservative leadership, so progressives must withhold certain political issues which might offend the community. This typical social-democratic paternalism is an insult to the political sophistication of the Black community.

The Trend's homophobia and anti-feminism, its Trotskyist-baiting and phony "race is primary" line, and its anti-democratic maneuverings in the mass movements have earned the organization the dubious honor of being recognized as one of the most disreputable forces within the Left today.

### Workers World Party

Workers World Party (WWP), a neo-Stalinist formation headed by arch-cultist and ex-SWPer Sam Marcy, supports Black cultural nationalism. WWP has also became increasingly known for its bureaucratic procedures and use of goon squads against those who disagree with their line on any issue. This despotism reached a peak during national preparations for the All People's Congress and at the congress itself, held in Detroit, Michigan from October 16-18, 1981.

The congress was organized by the WWP under the auspices of People's Anti-War Mobilization (PAM), an open coalition which had been taken over by WWP.

In Seattle, FSP and RW members and supporters were expelled from PAM for being "disrupters." FSP had challenged WWP's anti-democratic methods, and had openly disagreed with Black nationalists within the committee. How dare anyone challenge a Black person! How racist!

The shoe was on the other foot, though, at the All People's Congress, where WWP exposed the flipside of its fanatic support to the Black nationalists by provoking a racist incident. A Black male speaker was *forcibly removed* from the speaker's platform by WWP goons for espousing sexist and homophobic ideas.

**THE 1984 ELECTIONS**

MONEY FOR JOBS—NOT FOR WARS ABROAD
Fight Racism, Sexism, Lesbian & Gay Oppression!
workers world party

- Why Workers World Party is running candidates
- Why we also support the Jesse Jackson campaign
- A working class program to advance the fight for jobs, justice, and socialism and end imperialist war

*Workers World Party's opportunism was displayed when it rejected the socialist principal of opposing capitalist parties and backed Democrat Jesse Jackson for president solely because he was a popular Black candidate. (WWP campaign brochure.)*

So much for the right of free speech, healthy discussion, and the principled debate of ideas which most of the Left pretends to hold sacrosanct. Not the WWP—no free speech on the Left for them!

WWP's ejection of the Black speaker made *him* the problem and not his ideas. So much for their hallowed support of Black nationalism! So much for across-the-board support to anyone with nonwhite skin color! Their action illuminates the fact that WWP's "support" is really a cover for deep-seated racist contempt. It also reveals how quickly this contempt can beget the kind of violence once employed by Sheriff Bull Connor in Birmingham.

WWP's treachery and hysteria are dangerous signs of these tense times, when many radical groups are making wild and unpredictable turns, usually to the right.

WWP's dictatorial methods within the mass movements, its program of cultural nationalism, and its blatant sexism could quickly lead these chameleons down the road previously trod by Lyndon LaRouche's National Caucus of Labor Committees (U.S. Labor Party) as it raced to the ultra-right.

## The Communist Workers Party

The Communist Workers Party (CWP), which had five members murdered by Klan/FBI agents in Greensboro, North Carolina in 1979, maintains that the Black struggle is nationalist in origin and character. However, unlike most proponents of Black nationalism, the CWP gives some recognition to the revolutionary potential of Black feminism.

The CWP takes its nationalist analysis one step further by promoting a dangerous analysis of the nature of the Black petty bourgeoisie. The following summary is taken from the article "The State of the Black Liberation Movement" in the CWP newspaper, *Workers Viewpoint*:

> The Afro-American movement is a *multi-class* movement [emphasis added]. The national movements are the main allies of the working class in the struggle to overthrow U.S. Imperialism and establish worker rule in the U.S. All classes, the working class, the petty bourgeoisie and the national bourgeoisie suffer national oppression.[121]

True, the relationship of the Black petty bourgeoisie to the Black working class is influenced to some degree by race solidarity. And there are certainly stronger cross-class allegiances among Blacks than among whites. In the future, as class conflict deepens, a large percentage of the Black petty bourgeoisie may even ally with the working class.

Nevertheless, to offer across-the-board, uncritical support to the Black petty bourgeoisie and the Black *bourgeoisie* is ludicrous, superficial, and amounts to a liberal/racist view of the Black movement as an amorphous mass, devoid of concrete class differences.

Such an analysis plays directly into the hands of the ruling class.

### The "White European" syndrome

Nothing is odder and more ridiculous than the recent phenomenon on the Left of loud "anti-racist" whites who carry out support work for Black nationalist organizations.

The African People's Socialist Party (APSP) has a periphery of such people whom the APSP calls "White Europeans"! The APSP has created its own caste system: White Europeans run around organizing benefits and speaking engagements out of a heavy sense of guilt about their "wrong" heritage.

We first heard about White Europeans from the Black Muslims (hardly noted for scientific anthropology). Then Black nationalists leaped on the phrase to discredit *Marxists,* who supposedly didn't express the *African* experience in their writings and theory. The phrase was also applied to *Jews,* especially Jewish socialists. Today, Russell Means, Native American leader of the American Indian Movement, uses it in the same way to slander his own Marxist/Jewish supporters—knowing that most of them will *accept* the denunciation!

Behind this absurd formulation lurks anti-Semitism, red-baiting, and guilt manipulation. Not all Europeans are Anglo-Saxon. Millions of Black Africans are Marxists. Jews are not Caucasians but Semites. Marx and Engels were the *first* European scholars to explore African cultures and support African liberation. And neither skin color nor geography nor relatives determine the integrity and politics of an individual or a group.

The nationalists concoct stereotypes where no basis for a stereotype exists. And their white entourage laps it up. Curiouser and curiouser...

### The Black worker as stereotype: RWL and SL

Two Trotskyist organizations, the Revolutionary Workers League (RWL) and the Spartacist League (SL), have at least partially adopted FSP's program on Revolutionary Integration, and formally call themselves revolutionary integrationists.

RWL and SL both profess the belief that the question of Black liberation is integrally connected to the unification of the U.S. working class, and that racism is divisive to workingclass unity and a main deterrent to the forward motion of the U.S. class struggle. They believe that Black leadership is critical to the development of a revolutionary U.S. proletariat.

However, the failure of both organizations to grasp the revolutionary implications of the Woman Question limits their understanding of the Black movement. Through a denial of the key importance of feminism, both organizations are unable to understand the ability of the woman of color to connect the Black movement with the movements of other people of color and the labor movement. As a result, both organizations retain a one-dimensional and limited understanding of the struggle for Black freedom.

RWL's program on the question of Black liberation over-emphasizes the Black male industrial worker and fails to even mention the role of the Black woman within her community, within the feminist movement, or within the workplace. RWL refuses to acknowledge that sexism and racism work hand-in-glove to keep the working class divided. They lightly dismiss the importance of mass movement work (especially mass work that deals with feminist issues), and go for broke on union organizing.

RWL mechanistically views the "primary" class struggle as preeminent over the battle against sexism—as if sexism existed only outside the workplace and class struggle only existed *inside* the workplace.

The ultra-left Spartacist League regards feminism as class collaborationist by definition, because feminist issues span class lines and therefore, according to the SL, are divisive to the class struggle.

SL also tells anyone within earshot that affirmative action is a ruling-class plot, devised by the bosses as a union-busting tactic. Besides being arrogantly insulting to the women and people of color who have battled for years to win affirmative action *against the bosses' opposition,* the SL's through-the-looking-glass approach to affirmative action condemns women and people of color to no improvement in their status until *after* the revolution.

Both RWL and SL slight the movements of other people of color by an over-emphasis and unbalanced view of the importance of the Black worker. This simplistic approach to the race question in the U.S. writes off the revolutionary potential of the masses of non-white workers who are not Black, offers no program for the unification of workers of color, and ignores the fact that a large number of Black workers derive from family lines that are not fully Black.

The combination of blatant sexism and racist downplaying of non-Black people of color by the RWL and SL retards and inhibits class unity.

## Revolutionary Integration at work in the Black community

The history of the FSP's past and present intervention and relatively successful alliance with the Black community originated from the adoption of the Revolutionary Integration program and its application in the community.

The Seattle branch in the '60s had outstanding alliances and close collaborative working relationships with SNCC, the Black Student Union at the University of Washington, the Black Panther Party, Black women's groups, and others. Seattle FSP has since worked with United Workers Union-Independent, the Lesbians of Color Caucus, the Seattle Anti-Klan Network, and the Seattle Black Women's Network. Additionally, FSP and RW comrades organized the campaign to send people of color representatives from the Seattle area to the First National Third World Lesbian/ Gay Conference in Washington, D.C. in October 1979.

In Los Angeles, years of FSP work with the Committee Against Police Abuse have produced real respect for our consistency and integrity.

Similarly, the Portland FSP branch is a model because of its important interventions and the decided impact it has had in the Black community over a period of years.

It was the first national branch to hold a public forum on Michele Wallace's book, *Black Macho and the Myth of the Superwoman*. Many Blacks attended the July 1979 forum, and the discussion was lively and productive. The event was taped by a local radio station.

181

The Portland branch has consistently prioritized work with women of color and the comrades participate in organizations of Black women, Black lesbians, and lesbians of color. The branch publicly supports Portland's Black United Front (BUF) on survival issues affecting the Black community, but at the same time it is properly a vocal critic of BUF's nationalist directives, ultimatums, and decrees to white radicals.

Because of the branch's principled and clear position on nationalism, it has come under fierce attack by Black nationalists, opportunists, and conservatives, and it has waged a brave ideological and programmatic return battle.

These fights drew the lines within the party itself when a Black lesbian branch leader succumbed wholesale to nationalist pressures, left the organization, and has been slandering and fighting the branch ever since.

Undaunted by the divisiveness and demagogy of the nationalists and conservatives in the Black community, Portland excels in advancing Revolutionary Integration.

Unity in struggle with Black women and men has been won through the practice of socialist feminism, resulting in the recruitment of Black members to national RW and FSP, and the creation of good allies. Alliances with Blacks will expand and strengthen as the party holds strong to Revolutionary Integration, especially amidst the heated debates with Black nationalists.

## Crisis of leadership in the Black movement

Reaganite reaction has exacerbated the leadership crisis within the Black community itself. The Black nationalist and reformist elements that rose to the fore in the '70s are totally unequipped to deal with the nature and scope of the current civil rights rollback. Their pro-capitalist, anti-revolutionary programs are nothing but prescriptions for suicide.

Fresh leadership and programmatic alternatives are crying necessities for the Black movement. As new leaders arise, their search for allies against the right wing will quickly throw them into conflict with the nationalists and reformists. And their struggles against these dead-end misleaders will determine the shape—and the survival—of Black politics in the '80s.

### Threat of the cultural nationalists

Black nationalists today are scurrying around the country fanning the winds of reaction and appealing to disenchanted, middleclass Blacks.

Their program is a frightening combination of sexism, homophobia, anti-Semitism, anti-Marxism, and anti-workingclass dogma. The scenario is reminiscent of pre-WWII Germany, where the middle class was seduced into Nazism by male-supremacist, anti-Semitic, and mystical aspirations to upper-class status.

Most Black nationalists have a common enemy: Karl Marx and his "White European clones"—the U.S. Left.

Black nationalist author Shawna Maglangbayan profaned Black Marxists and class struggle when she wrote in 1973:

> Marxism-Leninism is a reactionary and white supremacist ideology whose chief aim is to maintain Aryan world hegemony once capitalism is overthrown. The idea of an "alliance" with Left-wing white supremacy is a stillborn infant which Black Marxist fanatics resuscitate each time they muster enough force to rear their heads in the Black community.[122]

Maglangbayan's ungrounded and illogical rhetoric is typical of nationalists who exist in a realm where falsehood is taken for reality. Their style echoes history's most hysterical propagandists: invoke panic and spur group isolation by incinerating "whitey" and anyone associated with whites. And their most virulent attacks are aimed at political principle and revolutionary ideology.

The nationalist demagogues also buy into bigotry against other oppressed groups.

According to Chicago psychologist Bobby Wright, Black lesbians and gays are reactionary contributors to racist genocide. Wright also labeled Michele Wallace as "sick and suicidal" because she dared expose Black male sexism in *Black Macho and the Myth of the Superwoman.*

Jews become scapegoats for Black rage. Stokely Carmichael, founder of the nationalist All-African People's Revolutionary Party, declared at an Arab student conference in 1974 that he had reversed his "former defense of Jewish people." Camouflaged by a phony, misapplied "anti-Zionism," Carmichael spouted rhetorical gibberish that amounted to little more than vulgar anti-Semitism. And he is not alone.

*Stokely Carmichael led SNCC toward an aggressively nationalist stance. He split with the Black Panther Party after fighting unsuccessfully to prevent its alliances with white radicals.*

A host of nationalists including Bobby Wright and Harold Cruse, a prolific writer and ex-member of the CP, have joined the anti-Semitic chorus and rabidly denounce *all* Jewish people.

They say that Jews are cohorts of the white imperialist enemy and that Jews are the archetypical white capitalist exploiters of the world's people of color!

However, these nationalist hypocrites are pro-capitalist themselves, and seem ready to foment pogroms in order to corner the ghetto market for *Black*-owned businesses. But they are not about to organize against the rulingclass monopolists who are really responsible for Black misery. Black business is, after all, mortgaged to big-time capital.

Earl Raab, a Jewish activist, writer, and professor, challenges nationalist anti-Semitism in his article "The Black Revolution and the Jewish Question":

> [Blacks] trying to reassure Jewish audiences repeatedly and unwittingly make the very point they are trying to refute. "This is not anti-Semitism," they say. "The hostility is toward the whites." When they say "Jew," they mean "white." But that is an exact and acute description of political anti-Semitism. The "enemy" becomes the Jew, "the man" becomes the Jew, the villain is not so much the actual Jewish merchant on the corner as the corporate Jew who stands symbolically for generic evil. "Don't be disturbed," the Jews are told, "this is just poetic excess." But the ideology of political anti-Semitism has precisely always been poetic excess, which has not prevented it from becoming murderous.[123]

The self-avowed, bigoted leaders of Black nationalism ignore the historic alliances between Blacks and Jews. Monica Hill, socialist feminist analyst of Middle Eastern

185

affairs, wrote in 1979:

> The majority of world Jewry is neither pro-Zionist nor middle class—nor tenement landlords nor pawnshop owners. Jewish radicals and humanists have always worked for—and died for—Black freedom... The White House *wants* Jewish and Black workers to battle each other instead of their common enemy—capitalist rule. So all Jews are blamed for Carter's apparent anti-Arab stance (just as all whites are wrongly blamed for racial segregation and ghetto poverty).[124]

Black nationalists rarely defend workingclass struggles, and, as noted, are most often bent on promoting *Black capitalism* within the community—on the pretext that if it's Black, it's good.

However, money passing through the hands of the Black consumer to a Black shop owner, rather than to the white proprietor, is hardly revolutionary. Nor does a change of the boss's color denote an end to exploitation.

The laws of capital are color blind. A boss is a boss, a worker a worker, and never the twain shall meet. Workers are exploited by the bosses, and in the final analysis, the bulk of the Black bourgeoisie will be true to its *class* interests before its race interests.

Characteristic of the nationalists is their utter refusal to openly and honestly discuss and debate ideas. A good case in point is the participation of the African People's Socialist Party at a "Fight the Right" forum on Black nationalism held in Seattle in November 1981. The APSP describes itself as Pan-African and a follower of Nkrumah.[125] And while they have disagreements with other Black nationalist groups, like the Republic of New Africa, over whether Blacks are Africans or constitute a separate nation on this continent, their avowal of race as the primary dividing line between peoples places them squarely in the camp of the cultural nationalists.

The following quote is taken from the APSP newspaper *The Burning Spear:*

> Another example of the Party's revolutionary leadership expressing itself through our mass work, was a forum held by FIGHT THE RIGHT on Black Nationalism, in which the political perspectives of African Liberation were put forth by the Republic of New Africa, the African People's Socialist Party and an Ideological Imperialist formation called the Freedom Socialist Party which unites with Imperialism by saying that African people in America became "free and American" and that we have always struggled for integration into American society. The APSP representative smashed this opportunist posture as well as the [Republic of New Africa's] BLACK BELT SOUTH THEORY, as the Party's line took clear command of the politics which many people afterwards expressed.[126]

As the unidentified "imperialist-opportunist" speaker who represented the FSP, I can tell you that what the *Burning Spear* article refers to is my presentation on the theory of Revolutionary Integration—a presentation that nowhere included the statement that Black people have become "free"!

The APSP's deliberate misrepresentation of the FSP's position is consistent with its equally dishonest account of its own participation in the night's events.

The APSP speaker's entire presentation consisted of reading non-programmatic rhetoric from the *Burning Spear* and proffering repeated assertions that Blacks, as "Africans," have nothing in common with white "North American" workers. The FSP's presentation was a distillation of the analysis and conclusions contained in this document. The APSP speaker, apparently unacquainted with the actual history of Black experience and struggle in this country, was ill-prepared to refute our contention that Blacks in the U.S. *are* Americans and that their struggle is integral and central to the American revolution as a whole.

Little debate, in fact, was mounted by the APSP in the discussion that followed the presentations. Why debate and risk total exposure when you can lay back and slander your opponent at a more convenient time?

Intervention such as FSP provided at the "Fight the Right" forum is more essential than ever. The danger in this period is that, as repression escalates, the absence of a revolutionary leadership that expresses race, class, and sex issues in the Black community will allow the nationalist impulse to expand. We will hear more lies and nonsense and gibberish and slander until the air is cleared by debate and theory is tested against theory where it counts—in *action.*

## The reformists

Black reformist leadership today is where it always has been—at the White House for a crisis-chat over lunch, or out pushing Operation Breadbasket and Push to Excel, or talking the same old drivel about trying the Republicans this week and the Democrats the week after.

The reformists, largely Black middleclass or professional and skilled labor, are mired in the pursuit of the good life and the green stuff. These poseurs, the Jesse Jacksons, the Andy Youngs, et al.—will never change.

But they can still be pressured into temporary leftward turns. They are desperately playing both ends against the middle. A strong Black movement will force them to move, as they scramble to maintain a base of support in the Black community, while assuring the Big Boys that they're on *their* side.

*The reformists have their own crisis of leadership.* They have no strong organizations and absolutely no program. They are leading no one anywhere. Ideologically bankrupt, defeated, and frightened, they will fight grimly to protect their privileges. And when the time is upon them to choose between their selfish class interests and the real interests and demands of Black people, they will become dangerous mercenaries in suits and ties—in a deadly battle against Black, and all other, revolutionaries.

## The masses

The situation for Blacks is a cause for grave alarm. As we have seen, Black people are leaderless and lack a politically effective program for action.

The crisis of leadership is not like that of 1965. It is much more serious. It is an appalling *absence* of leadership.

The situation demands leadership that is radical, bold, and revolutionary; that is determined to wipe out, once and for all, every trace of *every* oppression that is maiming Black people's—and all people's—lives.

Such leadership is brewing, down in the ranks.

The Black community is angry and it is gearing up to move. It will not suffer in silence the disquieting echoes of pre-fascist, lynch mob terror.

The 1980s were ushered in by the Miami riots. Miami blew up over the issue of police brutality but the underlying factors were the sheer poverty and dehumanizing racism of the ghetto.

Miami was only the most visible and dramatic expression of growing resistance.

When Ronald Reagan became the head of the latest White House mafia, Black people's inaugural greeting was the January 1980 Martin Luther King Memorial March in the nation's capital.

Protests have mounted against renewed attacks by the Ku Klux Klan and by the neo-fascists who roam the country storm-trooper style. Nationwide demonstrations sprang up over the mass murders of Black children in Atlanta.

New political organizations are developing to meet the new challenges and each must be evaluated for its strengths, its weaknesses, and its potential for leadership.

For example, there is the National Black United Front, headed by Herbert Daughtry, a Brooklyn minister. As the largest national Black grassroots organization, its purpose is to gain independence for Black people. But its politics are dominated by nationalist ideology, virulent sexism, sectarianism, and redbaiting hysteria, most blatant in its West Coast chapters.

The most principled new Black organization is the National Black Independent Party (NBIP), whose spokesperson is the Reverend Ben Chavis.

Chavis has an impressive history of militancy. In February 1971, he led Black protesters, mostly youths, in a citywide protest over discriminatory practices in the public high school of Wilmington, North Carolina. The National Guard moved in and shot and killed two of the protesters. Ten other protesters were arrested on trumped-up charges and sentenced to 24 years each in prison.

The cause of the "Wilmington Ten" became known across the country, and they were freed from prison in the late '70s through efforts of a national defense committee.

NBIP's program is anti-capitalist, anti-racist, and anti-sexist, and it has chapters in major metropolitan localities. Membership includes independents, nationalists, Stalinists, Maoists, and Trotskyists (SWP and Revolutionary Workers League). If NBIP sticks to its own program and organizes as an openly radical party, its future is promising.

Its difficulty will be in hammering out a democratic structure based on the principle of each component group's right to dissent and voice its differences. The issue of democracy will be a decisive factor in the survival and effectiveness of NBIP.

The crisis of leadership in the Black community is a challenge and an opportunity for Marxists. This leadership void can be filled by means of an open, wholesome struggle of ideas. But the opportunity for ideological debate must itself be fought for.

All the reformists, nationalists, and cultural gurus have failed miserably. They do not have a revolutionary program nor do they encourage or permit the free exchange of ideas and mutual support on common problems. Black people are looking for new ideas, a new course of action, and new allies; the door to the Black working class and the masses is wide open.

## Striking a blow for global freedom

The situation for Black people in America has never been more critical. Yet the Black community, in its essential internationalist spirit, is concerned with much more than its own grave situation. The struggle, for example, of southern African peoples to smash the chains of neo-colonialism is fervently supported in every U.S. Black community. The deportations and imprisonment of Haitians in U.S. concentration camps have likewise brought a cry of outrage.

Regardless of all the years of misleadership, worldwide Black revolutionary bonding is still a reality. Aided by modern technology and communications, the maturing global solidarity of Black people and of all people of color is a startling contemporary phenomenon. All people of color wage an ever vigilant life-or-death fight against the *common enemy* of imperialism and domestic capitalism.

Blacks around the world are determined to win nothing less than real freedom. They demand a complete end to human misery and want. It should not be necessary to starve and scramble to survive, and they know it. Millions of valiant Black warriors remain steadfast in the realization that such a goal cannot be achieved in isolation, but only through international comradeship, sisterhood, and fraternity.

People of color—a rainbow of power from Vietnam to El Salvador, from Oakland's Chinatown and Wounded Knee to the migrant labor fields of the Sacramento Valley—closely identify with and learn from the American Black liberation struggle. And while they learn, they also teach! As leaders of their own national, racial, and class wars of liberation, they teach U.S. Blacks the way to an international socialist society. They direct the course to a living, attainable, egalitarian future.

However, a people living for victory through struggle must develop the highest political awareness.

The fight against racism exists not only outside but *within* the communities of people of color.

The substitution of chauvinistic and separatist cultural nationalism for class struggle can only strengthen the concrete evils of capitalism within the various communities.

Separatist theoretical and tactical errors will pit Black against Brown against Yellow against Red, destroy critical political alliances, and allow sexism, homophobia, and a wholly anti-workingclass ideology to sneak in the back door.

Being swept up in racist and sexist antagonisms, with brothers battling brothers and sisters battling sisters, only sets the stage for the reformist middle caste—opportunist misleaders and traitors to the community—to rise to leadership and successfully hold back class struggle.

Revolutionary Integration—*assimilation* into revolution—is the Bolshevik feminist contribution to the theory and practice of global revolt! The Black Question is the key international question, as it is the key North American question. It is central to workers' struggles, national liberation struggles, the fight for democratic freedoms, and women's emancipation—in short, the entire world development of Permanent Revolution in our time.

## Black revolt and Permanent Revolution

Permanent Revolution is the worldwide, uninterrupted and uninterruptible struggle of all oppressed people, led by the proletariat, for economic, social, and political equality. Running like a connecting thread through the fabric of Permanent Revolution is irrepressible Black protest and revolution.

The theory of Permanent Revolution, first formulated by Marx and later extended and enriched by Lenin and Trotsky, states in essence that *the unfinished tasks of bourgeois democracy can only be completed by proletarian socialist revolution.*

Further, the Permanent Revolution is *international in character and scope,* and *all* democratic struggles are indissolubly bound up with the success of workers' revolution in the advanced industrial countries.

Permanent Revolution today takes aim at the capitalist state, its institutions, and the entire system of racist, sexist, and homophobic relations which hold bourgeois rule in place. It is a *total* revolution—at once economic, social, and political. Nothing less will free us once and for all from capitalism.

Black liberation in the U.S. and world socialist revolution are *mutually interdependent.*

Black people's struggle for equal rights in this country is a democratic struggle par excellence. But it cannot fully succeed within the framework of capitalism, which has from the beginning subsisted on racist inequality. The profit system continues to depend on the super-exploitation of Black labor and on the anti-Black racism that has historically divided the U.S. working class. There is no way that capitalism can allow Black equality.

Black liberation and survival are thus inextricably tied to

the success of socialist revolution. But, in turn, the revolution cannot succeed without Black struggle and leadership.

The U.S. Black movement is overwhelmingly a *workers'* movement inside the heartland of world imperialism. Black people are, and always have been, among the most oppressed and most militant of U.S. workers, the first to voice the demands and aspirations of the entire class, and the leading fighters against the segregation that divides and weakens all workers. Their struggle is a central rallying point for labor unity and, by that fact alone, is a death threat to capitalism.

The Black movement, moreover, inspires oppressed people all over the world: other people of color movements in this country, the feminist and lesbian/gay movements in every country, the nationally and racially oppressed from Northern Ireland to South Africa and Australia, and the socialist and labor movements in Asia, Latin America, Europe, and Africa.

In the U.S. and across the globe, at a thousand different points, Black liberation and Permanent Revolution mutually strengthen and enhance one another.

Isn't it significant that most Black African revolutionaries are internationalists and *not* cultural nationalists? U.S. Blacks who endlessly yearn after Africa and the "African Experience" hardly reflect or express Black Africa's opinion of the road to freedom for U.S. Blacks! The greatest act that Black Americans can engage in for the benefit of their African cousins is to lead the American revolution.

This is what the Black world expects of U.S. Blacks. And this is what American Blacks owe to themselves, to their people in global bondage, and to the entire human race. It is the intrinsic, necessary, and natural internationalism of American Blacks that will, in the final analysis, prove to be the salvation of society.

Let us seize the time! Through the continued advocacy

Lin Shi Khan/Tony Perez, 1935

*Freedom from race, sex and class oppression will come about only through social transformation grounded in Revolutionary Integration and socialist feminism.*

and application of the FSP program, we *can* seize the time!

The program of the FSP is a *living* and viable entity, not an ideal that is abstract and separate from the daily lives of Black people or from our daily lives as Marxists. The Black struggle is our struggle. Ours is the solution to the crisis of leadership in the Black community, and it calls for tenacity, tenacity, tenacity—and conviction!

## What must be done

The death agony of capitalism creates convulsions which strike hardest at the most vulnerable. And their resistance heats up the global class struggle to the boiling point.

We are approaching a new revolutionary age! We are in the dawn of the coming American revolution. Much can be done.

The present crisis of all the social movements compels the FSP to assert more boldly than ever its Bolshevik, socialist feminist principles. Revolutionary politics are the solution to the general crisis of leadership.

We must resolutely put forward the tenets of Revolutionary Integration in every facet of the race, sex, and class struggle. We demand political assimilation into revolution. And this agenda is as valid for Black people as for other working people.

Precisely *how* do we apply Revolutionary Integration at this political conjuncture? The theory itself supplies the guidelines to practice.

## Our general course

1. The theory and practice of Revolutionary Integration remains the solution to the Black Question. Revolutionary Integration is therefore fundamental to the program of the Freedom Socialist Party.

2. Party membership must continue the study of the Black Question and Black history, and attain a theoretical grasp of Revolutionary Integration versus Black nationalism. Our task is to constantly and patiently explain why and how the Black struggle is the key to the American Question and to the world revolution.

3. Socialist feminism must be interjected into all party work within the Black community and elevated to the first level of priority in our educational and recruitment activities.

4. The Third World lesbian/gay movement is integral to the unification of all the liberation movements. The party's connection with this movement must be sustained.

5. The popularization of the labor party slogan is critical to welding the struggles of Black workers with those of all workers into a mutually supportive class and race conscious-

ness. For the creation of a labor party based on the unions!

6. All party comrades must intensify their commitment to the Black struggle and actively seek to recruit Black members in the workplace and the community by prioritizing political work in this area.

7. Every branch and every comrade should stay alert to the daily issues and important events affecting the Black masses, and should continue personal and group involvement in actions, protests, and meetings in the Black community. The Black press should be studied and contributions made to it. Whenever possible we should take the initiative in organizing meetings and actions that advance the struggle.

8. The Comrades of Color Caucus of FSP and RW can become a more powerful vehicle for internal and external party building. It must serve as a leadership force among the general party membership, guiding the party as an educational and directive group. It must continue its national development. The CCC must reach out into the people of color communities: recruitment must be a top priority!

9. As party membership grows and matures, priority goals must be established for "colonization" and organizing in the Midwest, the eastern industrial centers, and the South.

### Emphasize the leadership role of Black women and Black lesbians and gays

Black history impels the Black woman into becoming the vanguard of her people. She is the connecting, unifying revolutionary link for the Black struggle and feminism, the Black struggle and labor, the Black struggle and anti-imperialism.

The Black woman, ever vigilant through two centuries of uncompleted revolution, has proven her innate capacity to furnish the necessary leadership for the American revolution. This process will be accelerated by the sheer determination and wisdom of the belittled Black "matriarch."

After centuries of struggle, the Black woman today is an even more powerful revolutionary force as a result of the dynamic emergence of the Black lesbian.

Black lesbians, the most harassed and reviled sector of people inside and outside the Black movement, are the most rebellious and the most unspoiled and creative radicals. They prove Lenin's dictum that the most tormented shall lead. The Black woman, the Black lesbian/gay, the Black worker, the Black rebel—all coalesce and become embodied in one person. Right on!

Power to the women people! Lesbians of color—take it away! The prospects for you are heady and limitless.

Nevertheless, the road to winning more Blacks to socialist feminism is steep and rocky. The urgent task of the party is to remain steadfast against, and critical toward, those regressive forces and illusions which many of our potential allies scurry toward: the creeping and pervasive lure of nationalism...the white/Black association conflict... narcissism...total dedication to seeking total sexual bliss... the comfort of respectable reformism...the vulgar rejection of *all* whites...the search for nirvana *now*.

White comrades are charged with the additional directive of confronting themselves, each other, and the mass movement about racist manifestations, practices, and language. White radicals can and must shed all vestiges of white guilt, liberal indulgence or color blindness, and ideological shallowness on the question of Blacks and people of color.

Black comrades and all comrades of color face a large task. They must confront and educate their communities against abounding intra-group egocentrism and rivalries. They must denounce in-group racism and sexism, so often glossed over and swept under the carpet. Lesbian sisters of color are the modern-day scapegoats and witches not only within the larger society, but in their own communities, which have yet to disavow male chauvinism, homophobia, and fundamentalist moralism.

It takes not only sensibility but sense, not only compassion but courage, to steer a direct course to freedom today. The Black lesbian, the ultimate rebel, can be vicious and neurotic—or she can be the most glowing revolutionary; it is ever thus with nonconformists and social critics. There is no middle road—this is the Age of Extremes!

## United front and multi-issue work

The key to winning allies and confidants in the Black struggle is the party's continued intervention into those issues which deeply affect the Black community.

The call for a united front is our most promising slogan for unifying Black, radical, feminist, and workingclass forces. Black issues are never *just* Black issues! The Black community instinctively realizes this, and the party knows this. Together we must teach it. To build class solidarity—to tackle fear and retreatism—this is the antidote to isolation, detachment, and despair.

## Organize for a labor party

Any united front action can serve to nourish the grounds for the formation of a labor party.

The call for a labor party, that mighty oppositional force to the twin parties of capitalism, is the searing necessity of the day.

A labor party whose membership is composed of workers and their allies, and whose leadership is representative of the most oppressed, will be the power to radically transform the slow-paced class consciousness of the U.S. working class.

A labor party that will eventually create soviets in the workplaces and institutions across America is not just a dream, but the logical organizational tool for the beginning mobilization of forces for the "Good Morning, Revolution" day.

Blacks think white workers will not join in solidarity with them. But that is wrong, historically, logically and practically wrong. Blacks think it is beneath their dignity to demand support from white workers, yet Blacks beg for concessions from the bosses or the government. The latter is a waste of time and dignity, the former is a valid approach *by* the dignified *to* their natural, if backward, allies.

Should the aroused and organized Black masses *demand* a labor party—or organize one themselves—white labor could not long resist.

The key to the building of a labor party is the involvement of Black workers, especially women. We must teach Blacks and whites alike to recognize the Black woman worker's enormous potential as a radical, political leader. And white radicals are central, not peripheral, in the process of cementing an alliance of Blacks, all other people of color, and whites.

Our agitation and organizing for the labor party is our best answer to the dead-end cultural nationalists!

### Slogans for the struggle

1. Stop U.S. government aggression against Blacks! Fight racism! Resist the KKK, the Nazis, and the white chauvinists! End police brutality!

2. For full economic, social, political, and cultural equality for Blacks!

3. Expand affirmative action in education, training, hiring, promotion, and seniority systems! No discrimination on the job!

4. Trade union organization of the Black worker!

5. Jobs for all! Free training and education for all! Decent public assistance grants! No utility shutoffs! Expanded public housing and house repair grants!

6. Independent Black political action through a Black

anti-capitalist party and through an American labor party!

7. End all discrimination against Black women and Black lesbians and gay men!

8. Defense of South African Blacks, Haitian refugees, and all Black victims of imperialism!

9. Solidarity with all oppressed and exploited people of color!

10. Freedom now through the united front of all fighters for Black liberation regardless of race, sex, sexual orientation, or political ideology!

11. Toward Black leadership in a united revolutionary struggle for a socialist America!

12. Black and workingclass liberation through socialist feminism!

# Afterword

The 1980s will be decisive for the Black movement and the entire American working class.

The future of all humanity depends upon what happens *now!* But there is only one way to create a society freed of the chains of race, sex, and class oppression. That will come about through a revolution grounded in Revolutionary Integration and socialist feminism. And it is these concepts and practices that will revolutionize U.S. workers and the popular masses.

The revolution *will* be achieved. Millions upon millions of workers are going to follow our course. They too will wake one fine morning and say, as Langston Hughes said:

Good morning, Revolution:
        You're the very best friend
        I ever had.
We gonna pal around together from now on...[127]

# Notes

1    The Montgomery, Alabama bus boycott erupted in 1955 after Rosa Parks (1913- ), a Black seamstress and officer in the local NAACP, refused to move to the "colored" section in the back of a bus. Martin Luther King, Jr. first attained national prominence as a result of his supportive role in this boycott, which lasted 382 days.

2    Little Rock, Arkansas was the site of violent white riots over school integration in 1957. Daisy Bates (1914-1999), an African American community leader, was the key figure in the uproar. She outmaneuvered state and city officials to keep nine Black children at Central High School. Bates received the NAACP's Spingarn Medal for her heroism in the crisis.

3    SNCC (Student Non-Violent Coordinating Committee) was the militant southern organization that led the integration fight in the 1960s. The formidable grassroots organizer Ella Baker (1903-1986) initiated SNCC's formation in 1960 in order to help youth break from the conservative approach of church-led groups such as the Southern Christian Leadership Conference (SCLC) and NAACP.

4    Robert Williams (1925-1996) was the fighting leader of Blacks in Monroe, North Carolina. He organized a nationwide defense of two Black children arrested in October 1958 on rape charges (the absurd and notorious "Kissing Case"). An articulate advocate of Black self-defense, Williams was later the victim of a crude police frame-up (described in Note 42).

5    Nothing since the Civil War equaled the intensity of the Black revolt of 1963. The slow pace of desegregation in the deep South was epitomized by Birmingham, Alabama and the rigid enforcement of segregationist policies carried out by the city's commissioner of public safety, Eugene "Bull" Connor.

In April, following his defeat in the race for mayor, Connor filed a legal challenge that allowed him to remain in office. The day after the elections, civil rights demonstrations began under the direction of Martin Luther King, Jr. and other church leaders. The demonstrations grew in size and intensity, despite the use of savage police dogs and powerful fire hoses against the demonstrators. Press photos of the ruthless police methods aroused national and international indignation.

In May, after five weeks of protest, the demonstrators had reached 3,000 and arrests numbered 1,000—half of them youngsters under 18 years of age.

President John F. Kennedy attempted negotiations through the office of his brother, Attorney General Robert Kennedy. African American leaders agreed to suspend demonstrations only if business leaders would desegregate lunch counters, increase employment opportunities for Blacks, release jailed demonstrators on signature bonds, and negotiate further social change through a biracial committee.

Three days after the truce, a Black leader's home and a Black-owned motel were bombed. A crowd of 2,500 Blacks attacked the Birmingham police and burned several stores and buildings. President Kennedy sent 3,000 federal troops, specially trained in riot control, to Birmingham.

The relative calm was shattered four months later on September 15, 1963, when racists bombed the Sixteenth Street Baptist Church during Sunday services. Four little girls were killed and many other children injured.

The revolt in Birmingham was the forerunner of uprisings in New York City's Harlem ghetto in 1964 and the Watts ghetto of Los Angeles in 1965.

6    Leroi Jones (1934 - ), poet-playwright turned Black nationalist, is now known as Imamu Amiri Baraka and is a self-described follower of "Mao Tse-tung thought."

7    Walker and Hargis were racist, fundamentalist, anti-labor, ultra-right southern demagogues active in opposing school integration. Major General Edwin A. Walker of the United States Army was stationed in Arkansas in 1957; Billy James Hargis was an evangelist and author of books on "Christian anticommunism."

8    James Meredith (1933- ), a war veteran, was the first African American to try to enroll in "Ole Miss," the University of Mississippi. The year was 1962.

9    Roy Wilkins (1901-1981) was the longtime national leader of the NAACP and spokesperson for the conservative and reformist wing of the Black movement.

10   That the drive for an independent labor party is inherent in the southern struggle was revealed in 1964, the year after this document was written, when the Mississippi Freedom Democratic Party was formed. Based on the overwhelmingly workingclass Black masses, the MFDP challenged the Democratic Party of Mississippi and the racial-political structure of the South, engendering tremendous impact on national politics. MFDP's revolutionary potential was largely ignored by Marxists, although liberal and "socialist" supporters of the Democrats worked overtime trying to destroy its independent character by keeping it within the national structure.

11  The CIO bureaucracy flinched at a head-on challenge to race segregation and confrontation with Democratic colleagues in the South. The "Operation Dixie" organizing drive of 1946-48 collapsed because the race issue was ducked.

12  The Taft-Hartley Act, passed in 1947, rolled back the gains labor had made under the New Deal. It outlawed closed shops and secondary boycotts, allowed states to pass "right-to-work" laws, permitted the U.S. president to declare mandatory "cooling off" periods during labor disputes, and required union leaders to swear they were not communists. Except for the anti-communist clause, most of its provisions still stand.

13  Emmett Till, a 14-year-old Black youth from Chicago who was visiting Money, Mississippi, was brutally murdered in August 1955 after a white woman accused him of whistling at her. Rather than suffer in silence, Till's mother put his body on display in Chicago so that people could see firsthand the reality of the lynch system. A quarter million people viewed Till's body. In cities throughout the U.S., tens of thousands rallied to protest the results of sanctioned racism; but President Eisenhower turned down a request to meet with Till's mother. The FBI refused to investigate the case, even though the murderers gave an interview to *Look* magazine. The killers were arrested and set free after a mock trial in September 1955.

14  The March on Washington Movement was organized in 1941 by A. Philip Randolph (1889-1979), founder and first president of the Brotherhood of Sleeping Car Porters (AFL). Denouncing the inadequacy of concessions to Blacks in the armed services and in war jobs, Randolph threatened to lead 50,000 Blacks to Washington, D.C. to protest opposition by Southern Railroad and others to the Fair Employment Practices Committee. To forestall the march, President Roosevelt issued an executive order mandating fair employment practices and Randolph cancelled the protest.

Randolph's long history as an organizer began toward the end of World War I with his founding of the socialist magazine, *The Messenger.*

15  Patrice Lumumba (1925-1961) was the founder of the Congolese Nationalist Party. He was elected prime minister when the Belgian Congo achieved independence in 1961 and the country was re-named Zaire. Lumumba opposed the Belgium-backed secession of Katanga province and was subsequently removed from office, jailed and murdered in 1961. The involvement of the CIA in his death has not been disproven.

16  The conservative nature of the African American middle class was a thesis developed at length by E. Franklin Frazier (1894-

1962), a sociologist whose major interest lay in the effect of race relations on social and economic status and the family. A socialist, Frazier promoted viewpoints that provoked criticism from both whites and Blacks. *The Negro Family in the United States, The Negro in the United States,* and *Black Bourgeoisie* are among the better known of his voluminous writings.

17    This description of national consciousness is a loose formulation by African American writer James Baldwin (1924-1987) that was adopted by the SWP majority for their 1963 resolution on the Black Question.

18    Joseph Stalin, *Marxism and the National Question: Selected Writings and Speeches* (New York: International Publishers, 1942), p. 12.

19    Leon Trotsky, *Stalin* (New York: Stein and Day, 1967), pp. 154-155.

20    The emergence and ebbing of the lesbian "separatists" in the 1970s parallels the short-lived turn of Blacks toward "nationalism" in the late 1960s and early 1970s. Black and female nationalism are equally doomed by the simple fact that neither sector, despite severe oppression, constitutes a nation.

21    Booker T. Washington (1856-1915) espoused accommodation to racism and segregation. He promoted industrial training for Blacks, rather than scholastic achievement. Militant Black intellectuals William Monroe Trotter (1872-1934) and W.E.B. DuBois (1863-1963) vociferously opposed Washington. In 1903, Trotter actually served a  month in jail for interrupting a public speech by Washington. Trotter and DuBois founded the Niagara Movement, which called for action against discrimination and led to the formation of the NAACP.

       DuBois initiated the idea that the 10% of Blacks who were educated, the so-called "Talented Tenth," was obligated to lead in advancing the race. The NAACP turned the concept into an orientation toward the Black elite. DuBois broke with the NAACP after many years of leadership because he disagreed with its legalistic focus. He was a socialist and Pan-Africanist.

22    The observation that a turn toward political action against the white power structure would provoke a radical, non-racialist tendency in the Nation of Islam was brilliantly confirmed shortly afterwards when Malcolm X (1925-1965) split from the Black Muslims. Inspired by the colonial revolution and the southern civil rights movement, he dropped race-separatism and adopted revolutionary and internationalist politics, seeking to orient the ghetto masses toward political struggle against the racist-capitalist system. Malcolm was assassinated in New York City on February 21, 1965. The gunmen were identified as Black Muslims, although Nation of Islam leader

Elijah Muhammad denied the complicity of his followers in the crime.

23  John Reed, "The World Congress of the Communist International," *The Communist* [U.C.P.], No. 10 (1920), pp. 2-3. Paraphrased in Theodore Draper, *American Communism and Soviet Russia: The Formative Period* (New York: Viking Press, 1960), pp. 320-321.

24  William Z. Foster (1881-1961), leader of a 1919 steel strike of 350,000 workers, collaborated with James P. Cannon (founder of U.S. Trotskyism) in the early days of the Communist Party. The Cannon-Foster faction struggled to proletarianize and Americanize the party. But Foster, more a unionist than a theoretician, succumbed to Stalinism, brought charges of Trotskyism against Cannon, and was instrumental in Cannon's expulsion from the CP. After World War II, Foster replaced Earl Browder as head of the party.

25  Earl Browder (1891-1973), general secretary of the CP from 1930 through World War II, was a classic puppet functionary for the Stalinists, typifying their policy of class collaboration. The tide turned at the end of the war when Jacques Duclos, French CP leader, was instructed by Stalin to denounce U.S. Communists for "excessive" class collaboration. The famous Duclos letter ended Browder's career; he was deposed, as a scapegoat, and then expelled in 1946.

26  Hugo Oehler (1903-1983) founded a sectarian grouping of U.S. Trotskyists in 1936. The Oehlerites had been expelled from the Workers' Party for violating party discipline in October 1935, after opposing on principle the temporary entry of the Workers Party into the Socialist Party. Trotsky advocated this "French Turn" because a large body of young leftwing workers and students had emerged within the Socialist Party worldwide.

27  *Leon Trotsky on Black Nationalism and Self-Determination* (New York: Pathfinder Press, 1967), pp. 10-19.

28  *Leon Trotsky on Black Nationalism and Self-Determination*, pp. 32, 57. Rosa Luxemburg, though herself Polish, opposed self-determination for Poland on the grounds that it was a reactionary and unrealistic demand.

29  Daniel Guérin, *Negroes on the March* (New York: Weissman, 1956), pp. 108-109.

30  We could add such categories as sex, age, sexuality, and physical condition to the aforementioned special groups who may desire autonomy in a workers state.

31  See James Baldwin's *The Fire Next Time* (New York: Dial Press, 1963), a powerful study of the race question.

32    The tactic of decertification suits against discriminatory union practices was first used in 1962 by the NAACP in a case involving the all-white Local 1 and the all-Black Local 2 of the Independent Metal Workers at the Hughes Tool Company in Houston, Texas. The two locals had been given joint certification by the National Labor Relations Board (NLRB) in 1959. In 1961, Local 1 refused to eliminate a discriminatory clause from the new contract proposal and signed an agreement with Hughes extending the old agreement. Local 2 and the NAACP filed a petition challenging the certification of Local 1. In February 1963, the NAACP requested a ruling from the NLRB that would make certification of unions contingent upon whether they represented all employees "without prejudice or discrimination."

Similar suits were filed against the Seafarers International Union in San Francisco and Local 2401 of United Steelworkers of America in Atlanta.

33    In May 1963, thousands of Blacks picketed construction sites in Philadelphia to protest the Jim Crow hiring practices of some of the building trades unions. During six days of picketing—including a 21-hour sit-in at the mayor's office—the men, women, and children of the ghetto continued their militant demonstration even in the face of brutal attacks by police. A handful of skilled Black workers was hired and the tactic was used again many times by organizations such as CORE (Congress of Racial Equality) and the NAACP.

34    Rev. Adam Clayton Powell, Jr. (1908-1972) became New York City's first Black councilman in 1941 and in 1945 became the first African American from the Northeast to be elected to Congress. He was re-elected to the House of Representatives nearly two-dozen times by Harlem voters. He was a flamboyant character and a gadfly on civil rights issues in Congress, but could also be highly unprincipled. In 1960, he successfully pressured Martin Luther King to call off a picket of the Democratic Party Convention by threatening to tell the press that King and gay civil rights and labor organizer Bayard Rustin (1902-1987) were having a homosexual affair.

35    Samuel Gompers (1850-1924) was a founder of the American Federation of Labor (AFL) and in 1886 became its first president, a position he held, except for one year, until his death. He was politically conservative, hostile to socialists, and dedicated to narrow, craft unionism that served the aristocracy of labor.

36    Ralph Bunche (1904-1971) joined the U.N. Secretariat in 1947 and won the Nobel Peace Prize in 1950 for brokering a truce between Arab nations and Israel. He was under-secretary of the

UN from 1955 to 1971 and participated in civil rights marches in the South during the 1960s. He opposed Martin Luther King's attempt to link the civil rights struggle and the movement against the war in Vietnam.

37 The American Labor Party (1936-1956) was a statewide New York formation to garner votes for Franklin Delano Roosevelt and other Democrats from socialists and radical unionists who did not want to endorse the state's Democratic Party machine.

38 William Worthy (1921- ) was a groundbreaking African American foreign correspondent for CBS television news. In the 1950s and '60s, he defied U.S. travel bans and seizure of his passport to report on events from inside China, Cuba, North Vietnam, Cambodia, and Indonesia. He launched the Freedom Now Party in 1963 at the March on Washington and chapters were also formed in Black communities in Detroit, Chicago, Cleveland, San Francisco, Los Angeles, New York, Seattle, and other cities.

39 See Robert Vernon, "White Radicals and Black Nationalism," *International Socialist Review* 25, no.1 (1964).

40 The Congress of Racial Equality (CORE) was formed in 1942 by James Farmer (1920-1999) to pursue social change through "nonviolent direct action." CORE's program of direct action was designed as a conscious alternative to the more passive, legalistic approach of the NAACP. During the 1940s, CORE led interracial groups in well-publicized sit-ins at Jim Crow restaurants, notably in Chicago. In the 1950s, CORE functioned in cooperative actions with other protest organizations and with unions.

CORE was eclipsed in the 1960s by Martin Luther King, Jr. and his activities. James Farmer was still national director of CORE in 1963 when *Revolutionary Integration: Dialectics of Black Liberation* was written. In later years, CORE, under the leadership of Roy Innis, espoused Black nationalism.

41 The Freedom Rides were first organized in May 1961 by CORE to test segregation of interstate buses and bus terminal facilities such as lunch counters and restrooms. Black and white college students, ministers, and professionals from northern cities rode the buses to Alabama where they were met by violence. One of the buses was burnt and a dozen persons were hospitalized. Those that continued on to Birmingham were met by street fighting. In Montgomery, a mob of 1,200 surrounded the Freedom Riders in a church and U.S. Attorney General Robert Kennedy was forced to send 400 federal marshalls to protect them. Leaving Montgomery for Jackson, Mississippi, the riders were escorted by 1,000 Ala-

bama national guardsmen. By August, 300 Freedom Riders of both races were serving terms at a Mississippi prison farm or out on bond pending appeal.

In response to these events, the federal government obtained rules outlawing segregation in interstate transportation facilities. First compliance came with bus companies, then railroads and airports.

42     In 1961, Robert Williams was framed on a phony kidnapping charge in Monroe, North Carolina. Threatened by southern "justice" and a "capture and kill" order of the FBI, Williams escaped to Cuba.

The Committee to Aid the Monroe Defendants was established to defend four other freedom fighters subsequently indicted for the fraudulent kidnapping. CAMD split when African Americans in the group, obviously seeking maximum support in the ghetto, insisted that the committee be all Black, while SWP representatives were equally adamant that CAMD be broad, all-inclusive, and non-political. The African Americans formed the Monroe Defense Committee, and MDC and CAMD carried out competitive, confusing and none too cordial campaigns to help the Monroe victims.

The SWP branches made CAMD a central activity, expending a tremendous amount of time and money in defense work. But when the case came to court, the four defendants refused CAMD help. It was a major failure of SWP policy, but it was never analyzed by the leadership, never explained to the members, and remains shrouded in mystery.

43     Leon Trotsky, *The First Five Years of the Communist International*, 2nd ed., vol. 2 (New York: Monad Press, 1972), pp. 355-356. Poet and novelist Claude McKay (1890-1922) is one of the unsung gay leaders of the Black and radical movements.

44     Leon Trotsky, *Writings of Leon Trotsky*, (New York: Pathfinder Press, 1973), p. 112.

45     Published as Robert Vernon, "White Radicals and Black Nationalism," *International Socialist Review* 25 no. 1 (1964): 5-10.

46     J.R. Johnson was the political pseudonym of C.L.R. James, a West Indian Trotskyist and author of many books including *The Black Jacobins* and *World Revolution 1917-1936*. James was part of SWP discussions with Trotsky on strategies for African American liberation and wrote the 1948 SWP resolution on the Black struggle. Johnson left the SWP with the Shachtmanites in 1940, returning in 1947. He left the party again in 1951 for undisclosed reasons.

47    Denying Southern congressmen their seats because their state governments were illegal products of the overthrow of Reconstruction was exactly the demand placed upon Congress by the Mississippi Freedom Democratic Party in 1965, two years after this resolution was presented to the SWP. The MFDP mobilized tremendous support for the issue in the South and North alike, even forcing Democratic congressmen from largely Black areas to support them. The SWP was absolutely unprepared for such a demand and played no part whatever in the campaign.

48    Erisa Moore, "The Bicentennial Celebration-Aberration," *Black Scholar* 7 (1976): 30.

49    James P. Cannon, *The First Ten Years of American Communism* (New York: Pathfinder Press, 1972), p. 234.

50    Ibid., p. 234.

51    Leon Trotsky, *The First Five Years of the Communist International,* 2nd ed., vol. 1 (New York: Monad Press, 1972), pp. v-vii.

       Great programmatic and practical gains were made in the first four congresses of the Comintern between 1919-1922. With Lenin's death and the gradual consolidation of Stalin's bureaucratic power, the Comintern degenerated steadily until its demise after the Seventh Congress in 1935.

52    Philip A. Foner, *Organized Labor and the Black Worker, 1619-1973* (New York: International Publishers, 1974), p. 163.

53    V.I. Lenin, *Selected Works,* vol. 10. (New York: International Publishers, 1938), p. 235.

54    Granville Hicks, *John Reed: The Making of a Revolutionary* (New York: Macmillan, 1936), p. 392.

55    *Leon Trotsky on Black Nationalism and Self-Determination,* p. 61.

56    See p. 62.

57    "The Black Struggle," *International Socialist Review* (Supplement to *Militant)* (11 December 1981): 4.

58    Ibid., p. 4.

59    Ibid., p. 5.

60    Ibid., p. 8.

61    Joseph Stalin, *Marxism and the National Question* (New York: International Publishers, 1942), pp. 12-13.

62    Megan Cornish, "The National Question in the United States," *FSP Pre-Convention Bulletin,* No. 17 (27 June 1982): 3.

63    Ibid., p. 5.

64    Ibid., p. 5.

65  *Militant* (May 1929) [no page given].

66  *Leon Trotsky on Black Nationalism and Self-Determination*, pp. 10, 11, 15.

67  Ibid., p. 11.

68  Ibid., p. 13.

69  Ibid., p. 18.

70  The Communist Party led the formation of the Sharecroppers Union in 1931. By 1935, the Alabama union had grown to nearly 10,000 members. Despite intense harassment by segregationists, it lasted until 1939.

71  *Leon Trotsky on Black Nationalism and Self-Determination*, p. 54.

72  George Breitman, "Freedom Now," *International Socialist Review* 24 (Fall 1963): 106.

73  A. Philip Randolph, "Why I Would Not Stand for Reelection as President of the National Negro Congress," *American Federationist* 48 (July 1940): 24-25.

74  Foner, *Organized Labor and the Black Worker*, p. 242.

75  Ibid., p. 184.

76  Daniel Guérin, *Negroes on the March*, p. 121.

77  Ibid., p. 131.

78  Ibid., p. 126.

79  Ibid., p. 131.

80  J.R. Johnson, "Negro Liberation Through Revolutionary Socialism," *Fourth International* (May-June 1950): 90-96.

81  Breitman, "Freedom Now," p. 107.

82  Clara Fraser, "FSP National Committee Discussion," transcript (December 1981), p. 25.

83  Guérin, *Negroes on the March*, p. 183.

84  Cannon, *The First Ten Years of American Communism*, p. 242.

85  See pp. 74-75.

86  Breitman, "Freedom Now," p. 107.

87  Fraser, "FSP National Committee Discussion," p. 24.

88  Clara Fraser and Richard Fraser, *Crisis and Leadership* (Seattle: Red Letter Press, 2000), p. 175.

89  Breitman, "Freedom Now," p. 107.

90  "A Transitional Program for Black Liberation," *International Socialist Review* 30 (November-December 1969): 67-68.

91  Jack Barnes, et al., *Prospects for Socialism in America* (New York: Pathfinder Press, 1976), p. 183.

92  Ibid., p. 175.

93  Jesse Jackson (1941 - ), Ralph Abernathy (1926 - 1990), and Andrew Young (1932 - ) all started out with Martin Luther King, Jr. in SCLC and moved increasingly into the mainstream. Jackson, after twice trying unsuccessfully to gain the Democratic Party nomination for president, became a freelance powerbroker in the party. Abernathy succeeded King as president of SCLC and promoted Black economic self-development; he endorsed Republican Ronald Reagan for president in 1980. Young served in the U.S. House of Representatives from 1973-77, became a UN delegate, and was mayor of Atlanta from 1982-90.

94  Sara Evans, *Personal Politics* (New York: Random House, 1979), p. 83.

95  Ibid., p. 87.

96  Ibid., p. 91.

97  Ibid., p. 91.

98  Julius Lester, *Revolutionary Notes* (New York: Grove Press, 1969), p. 177.

99  Fraser and Fraser, *Crisis and Leadership,* pp. 64-65.

100 Truman Nelson, *People with Strength: The Story of Monroe, N.C.* (New York: Marzani and Munsell, no date), p. 24.

101 Ibid., p. 27.

102 *Leon Trotsky on Black Nationalism and Self-Determination,* pp. 42-43.

103 Foner, *Organized Labor and the Black Worker,* p. 337.

104 Ibid., p. 390.

105 Ibid., p. 390.

106 The Dodge Revolutionary Union Movement (DRUM) and the Eldon Avenue Revolutionary Union Movement (ELRUM) are discussed in *Detroit: I Do Mind Dying* by Dan Georgakas and Marvin Surkin. (New York: St. Martin's, 1975).

107 June Jordan, "Poem on the Murder of Two Human Being Black Men, Denver A. Smith and Leonard Douglas Brown, at Southern University, Baton Rouge, Louisiana, November 1972," *Black World* 22 (March 1973): 65.

108 Manning Marable, "Black Nationalism in the 1970s: Through the Prism of Race and Class," *Socialist Review* 10, no. 2/3 (March-June 1980): 58.

109 Cornish, "The National Question in the United States," p. 8.

110 Angela Davis, "Reflections on the Black Woman's Role in the Community of Slaves," *Black Scholar* 3, no. 4 (December 1971): 14-15.

111 Gloria T. Hull, Patricia Bell Scott, and Barbara Smith, eds., *But Some of Us are Brave* (Old Westbury, NY: The Feminist Press, 1982), p. 19.

112 *Kinder, kirche, küche*—children, church, kitchen—was the Nazi slogan describing the proper sphere of womanhood.

113 Cherríe Moraga and Gloria Anzaldua, eds., *This Bridge Called My Back* (Watertown, MA: Persephone Press, 1981), pp. 126-27.

114 Combahee River Collective, "A Black Feminist Statement," *But Some of Us are Brave*, p. 14.

115 Ibid., p. 12.

116 Audre Lorde, *From A Land Where Other People Live* (Detroit: Broadside Press, 1973), p. 39.

117 L.N. [Lorraine Hansberry Nemiroff], letter to the editor in *The Ladder, 1957-1972.* Reprinted in 8 vols. (New York: Arno Press, 1975) vol. 1, no. 11: 26-30.

118 Robert Crisman, "History Made," *Freedom Socialist* 5, no. 4 (Winter 1979/80): 7.

119 Maria H. Dolan, "Atlanta Vertigo: A Dispatch From the Front," *Gay Community News* [Boston] 9, no. 35 (27 March 1982): 5.

120 Pat Parker, "Where Will You Be?" *Conditions: Five* (1979): 128-132.

121 Douglas Layne, et al., "The State of the Black Liberation Movement," *Workers Viewpoint* (28 October-4 November 1981): 6.

122 Shawna Maglangbayan, *Garvey, Lumumba and Malcolm: Black National-Separatists* (Chicago: Third World Press, 1973), p. 103.

123 James Baldwin, et al., *Black Anti-Semitism and Jewish Racism* (New York: Schocken Books, 1970), pp. 31-32.

124 Monica Hill, "Blacks vs. Jews: The Myth and the Reality," *Freedom Socialist* 5, no. 4 (Winter 1979/80): 10.

125 Kwame Nkrumah (1909-1972) was a socialist and pan-Africanist leader. He was the first president of Ghana, the earliest British colony in Africa to gain independence. In 1966, he was deposed by a military coup that was aided by the CIA.

126 "APSP Showing the Way in Seattle," *Burning Spear* 8, no. 9 (December 1981): 3.

127 Langston Hughes, *Good Morning, Revolution* (New York: Lawrence Hill, 1973), p. 3.

# Index

## A

Abernathy, Ralph  135, 213
Abolition movement  41
Abortion  160, 172
Affirmative action  152, 154, 172, 180, 200
AFL-CIO  148–149, 149–150, 150, 153
"Africa for the Africans"  40, 47
African liberation  179, 191
African People's Socialist Party (APSP)  178, 186–188
AFSCME, Local 1773  152
All People's Congress  175–177
All-African People's Revolutionary Party  184
American Colonization Society  41, 42, 44
American Federation of Labor (AFL)  62, 66, 98, 116, 118, 208
American Indian Movement  179
American Labor Party  66, 209
American Nazi Party  130
American Revolution of 1776  41
Anti-capitalist program  144
Anti-communism/redbaiting  62, 63, 118, 129, 175, 179, 183
Anti-Semitism  46, 179, 183, 184–186
Aptheker, Herbert  107
Assimilation  32, 39, 60, 92, 124
Atlanta, GA child murders  168–169, 190
Autonomy  156–157

## B

"Back to Africa" movements  41, 42, 43, 50, 112–113
Baker, Ella  65, 136, 203
Baldwin, James  19, 56, 76, 206
Barnett, Governor Ross  24–25
Barnett, Ida B. Wells  161
Bates, Daisy  203
Birmingham, AL desegregation

battles  16–17, 20, 22, 24, 47, 77, 203–204, 209
"Black Belt" thesis  50, 105–107, 109, 187
Black bourgeoisie  39, 44, 178
Black business  44, 46, 185, 186
Black church  15, 16, 19, 48, 65
Black culture  57–60
Black history  39–40, 46, 47, 56, 60, 83, 196
Black lesbians and gays  161, 166–171, 182, 184, 198, 210
Black middle class/petty-bourgeoisie  31–32, 109, 134, 152, 177–178, 183
Black migration to the North  43, 63, 107, 115
Black movement  92, 93–94, 99, 120, 122, 128, 133–134, 141, 156, 159, 161, 171, 172, 173, 179–180, 201; and independent politics  64–67, 200; Black vanguard party  67; Forty-ninth State Movement  44; government repression of  121, 133–134, 138, 143, 146; internationalism of  16, 40, 47–48, 93, 144, 191–192, 194; leadership crisis  18, 19, 31–33, 57, 94, 127, 134, 182–183, 189, 191; Niagara Movement  206; reformism in  16, 17, 18, 20, 30, 32, 33, 45–46, 56, 63, 64, 74, 134–136, 140, 155, 182–183, 188–189, 204; revolutionary direction of  15, 16, 17, 19, 26, 57, 93, 126, 128, 142; sexism in  138, 139–140, 160, 162, 174. *See also Civil rights movement*
Black movement in the North  18–19, 28, 30–31, 32, 57, 61, 64, 137; relations with socialist organizations  18, 85–86
Black movement in the South

15–18, 30, 32, 57, 137; strategies 17–18, 26–27, 83, 86. *See also Civil rights movement*
Black Muslims 18–19, 45–48, 74, 75, 129, 130–131, 136, 178, 206
Black nationalism/separatism 19, 33, 35–36, 39, 42, 44–46, 50, 53, 54, 76, 82, 92, 99, 122–123, 124, 130, 133, 136, 137, 155, 156–160, 176, 178–179, 182–188, 190, 192, 206; anti-Marxism of 133, 178–179, 190; anti-Semitism of 179, 184–186; as proposed by leftists 50–51, 52–53, 66, 70, 107, 113–114, 134, 175, 177; male chauvinism of 158–159, 160, 163–164, 183, 190; "nationalism" as synonym for militancy 41, 53, 56–57
Black Panther Party 107, 132, 142–144, 158, 181, 184
"Black Power" 137, 140, 141, 156, 157
"Black Pride" 157
Black Question (strategy for Black liberation) 37, 38–40, 83, 97, 109, 110, 173, 192, 196
Black socialists/communists 33, 44, 68, 70, 71, 72–73, 81, 87, 118
Black Star Line 43
Black Student Union 132, 181
Black vanguard party 86
Black women 115, 129, 135, 138–140, 142, 153, 154, 159–166, 180, 181, 197–198, 200
Black workers 15, 16, 19, 26, 30, 32–33, 45, 61–62, 63–64, 87–88, 95, 99, 110, 112, 115–116, 127, 134, 148–150, 152–153, 178, 180–181, 194, 196, 200; demands of 63, 101, 148, 149, 154; during WWI 42, 43; union caucuses 63, 154
Black Workers Congress 155

Black youth 15–16
Bolshevik Party 55, 95, 97, 102, 127
Boot, Tom 12, 91
Bourgeois democracy 21–22
Breitman, George 75, 113–114, 122, 127, 128, 129
Brotherhood of Sleeping Car Porters 44, 116, 117, 149, 205
Browder, Earl 51, 207
Bunche, Ralph 66, 208

**C**

Cannon, James P. 95, 97, 104, 105, 130, 207; opposition to Black nationalism 126
Capitalism 21, 58, 186, 191, 192, 193, 195; reliance on racism in U.S. 23, 37–38, 39, 92, 124, 193
Carmichael, Stokely 139, 140–141, 156, 157, *184*
Carter, President Jimmy 167
Castro, Fidel 31
Charleston, SC hospital strike 153–154
Chavis, Ben 190
Chisolm, Shirley 163
Civil Rights Act of 1964 150–151, 154
Civil rights movement 16, 28–29, 32, 64, 134, 135, 148, 150, 151, 152, 155, 206; women in the 138–140. *See also Black movement in the South*
Civil War 37, 58
Clark, Sheriff Jim 151
Class struggle 29, 38, 44, 92, 102, 103, 109, 121, 124, 126, 156–157, 175, 179, 180
Colonialism 40, 100, 124
Comintern (Communist, or Third, International) 35, 49, 50, 97–101, 102, 104–105, 111, 211
Committee Against Police Abuse 181
Committee to Aid the Monroe Defendants 78, 210

Communist League of America 51, 105, 107–111; slogan for Black movement 110

Communist Party (CP) - U.S. 12, 30, 33, 49, 50, 51, 68, 96, 97, 105, 106, 107, 111, 114, 118–120, 173–174, 207, 212; "Black Belt" thesis 50, 105–107, 108

Communist Party - Germany 104–105, 111

Communist Workers Party (CWP) 177–178

Congress of Industrial Organizations (CIO) 28, 30, 44, 62, 105, 205

Congress on Racial Equality (CORE) 75, 121, 208, 209–210

Connor, Eugene "Bull" 203

Convention Movement 42

Cornish, Megan 102, 157

Cox, Oliver C. 37

Cruse, Harold 185

Cuba 25, 27

Cultural nationalism 155, 156, 157, 158, 165, 175, 187, 192. *See also Black nationalism/ separatism*

Cumming, Clyde 128

**D**

Daughtry, Herbert 190

Davis, Angela 107, 159, 174

Democratic Party 62, 64–65, 66, 133, 139, 140, 173, 188, 204, 205, 209, 211

Detroit, MI 31, 152, 154

Dobbs, Farrell 128, 129

Dodge Revolutionary Union Movement 154

Drug and Hospital Workers Union, Local 119B 153

DuBois, W.E.B. 42, 48, 60, 206

**E**

Eisenhower, President Dwight 24, 25, 205

Eldon Avenue Revolutionary Union Movement 154

Engels, Frederick 179

**F**

Fair Employment Practices Committee 117, 205

Fanon, Franz 159

Farmer, James 209

Fascism 21, 22, 23, 110–111, 190

FBI 133, 136, 138, 146, 177, 205

Federal troops to the South 23–25, 77, 209

Feminism 160, 161, 162–163, 164, 174, 175, 179–180, 197; of Black women 160–165, 171, 177; white, middleclass feminism 162–163, 164

Foner, Philip S. 118

Forman, James 140

Foster, William Z. 51, 97, 207

Fourth International 111

Fraser, Clara (Kaye) 10, 12, 123, 126, 141, 159

Fraser, Richard (Kirk) 10, 12, 15, 69, 91, 123–124

Frazier, E. Franklin 37, 83, 205

Freedom Now Party 209

Freedom Rides 75, 145, 209

Freedom Socialist Party (FSP) 12, 13, 15, 91, 95, 102, 132, 165, 168, 171, 176, 179, 181, 182, 187–188, 195, 196–197; Comrades of Color Caucus 197; Los Angeles branch 181; Portland branch 181–182; Seattle branch 181

**G**

Garvey, Marcus 43–44, *45*, 46, 47, 50, 112

Garvey Movement 42, 44, 47–48, 50, 113

Germany 110, 118, 183

Gompers, Samuel 66, 79, 208

Gregory, Dick 59

Guérin, Daniel 118, 120, 121, 124, 125

**H**

Haitian immigrants 191

Hamer, Fannie Lou *65*, 140

Hamilton, Charles V. 156
Hansberry, Lorraine 19, 166
Hargis, Billy James 23, 204
Harlem 31, 42, 43, 44, 204
Harlem Renaissance 59
Harper, Frances W. 161
Hickman, James 120
Hill, Monica 185
Hinojosa, Claudia 167
Homophobia 168–169, 170,
174, 175, 183, 192
Hughes, Langston 201

**I**

Imperialism 103, 124, 191
Industrial Workers of the World
(IWW) 49, 82, 96, 97
Integration 31, 39, 49, 51, 52,
54, 56, 60, 73, 92, 107, 116,
122, 124, 132, 144; reformist
31–32, 33, 60
International Longshoremen's &
Warehousemen's Union 125,
153
Internationalism 57, 100–101,
103, 104
Ireland 98

**J**

J.P. Stevens Co. 153
Jackson, Jesse 135, 176, 188,
213
James, C.L.R. (J.R. Johnson) *80*,
81, 111–112, 210
Jewish Question (strategy for
Jewish liberation) 55
Jews 55, 113, 184–186
Jim Crow laws 58, 116, 137
Johnson, James W. 37, 121–122
Jones, Leroi (Imamu Amiri
Baraka) 17, 204
Jordan, June 155

**K**

Kennedy, Florynce 163
Kennedy, President John F. 16,
24–25, 204
Kennedy, Robert 204, 209
Kenya 40
Kerry, Tom 128, 129

King, Coretta Scott 153
King, Jr., Martin Luther 73, 107,
127, 134–135, 137, 150, 151,
152–153, 203, 208, 209, 213;
opposition to Vietnam War
135
"Kissing Case" 144, 203
Ku Klux Klan (KKK) 20, 24, 43,
120, 130, 144, 145, 151, 177,
190

**L**

Labor movement 44, 45, 61–64,
82, 87–88, 97, 99, 120, 126,
134, 135, 144, 147–148, 150,
151, 152, 154, 172, 180, 197;
bureaucracy 18, 28, 29, 32,
61–63, 107, 147; northern 18,
27–29, 154; racism in 27, 28,
61–63, 79, 96, 148, 150,
154; southern 27, 28–29
Labor party 66, 196–197, 199–
200, 201; in the South 27, 29,
204
Lambda 168
LaRouche, Lyndon 177
League of Revolutionary Black
Workers 154–155
Left (Trotskyist) Opposition 104–
105, 107, 111
Lenin, Vladimir I. 34, 53, 95, 97,
98, 99, 100, 101–104, 105,
193, 198, 211
Lesbians and gays 174, 175; of
color 166–168, 169, 170–
171, 182, 196, 198, 210. *See
also Black lesbians and gays*
Lesbians of Color Caucus 181
Lester, Julius 141
Liberia 43
Little Rock, AR integration riots
15, 24, 25
Liuzzo, Viola 151
Locke, Alain 37
Loeb, Mayor Henry 152
Lumumba, Patrice 31, 205
Luxemburg, Rosa 51, 207

**M**

Maglangbayan, Shawna 183–184

Malcolm X  86, 130, 136, 140, 142, 206
Male supremacy  46, 111
March on Washington for Jobs and Freedom  149, 150
March on Washington Movement  30, 116–117, 205
Marcy, Sam  175
Martin Luther King, Jr. Memorial March  189
Marx, Karl  179, 193
Marxism  33, 34, 35, 83, 86, 87, 88, 89, 165
McKay, Claude  35, 79, 210
McNair, Governor Robert E.  153
Means, Russell  179
Meany, George  150
Mejia, Max  167
Memphis, TN sanitation strike  125, 134, 135, 152–153
Meredith, James  24, 25, 204
Miami, FL riots  189
Militant, The  75, 77–78, 85, 121
Mississippi Freedom Democratic Party (MFDP)  65, 107, 140, 204–205, 211
Monroe Defense Committee  78
Monroe, NC  16, 21, 144–145, 146, 203, 210
Montgomery, AL  15, 16, 21, 30, 209
Montgomery, AL bus boycott  107, 134, 135, 137, 203
Moore, Erisa  94
Moynihan, Daniel  139–140, 158
Moynihan Report  139
Muhammad, Elijah  45, 74, 76, 129, 130, 207

N
Nation of Islam. See Black Muslims
National Association for the Advancement of Colored People (NAACP)  9, 15–16, 30, 42, 43, 44, 71–72, 78, 121, 144–145, 203, 206, 208, 209
National Black Independent Party  133, 190–191

National Black United Front  182, 190
National Caucus of Labor Committees  177
National Coalition of Black Gays  167
National Guard  151, 153, 190
National Lesbian/Gay March on Washington  166, 167, 168
National Negro Congress  71
National Third World Lesbian/Gay Conference  166, 181
National/Colonial Question (strategy for liberation)  34, 35, 38–39, 98, 99, 101–104, 105
Nationalism  33–34, 36, 53, 171. See also Black nationalism/separatism; Self-determination, right of nations to
Nationhood, defined  33, 35, 102–103, 110; national minority characteristics  109
Nazism  110, 183
Negro American Labor Council  63, 149–151
Nelson, Truman  22, 145, 146
Newton, Huey P.  142, 143
Newton, NC  144, 145, 146
Nkrumah, Kwame  186, 214
Norton, Eleanor Holmes  162

O
Oehler, Hugo  51, 207
"Operation Dixie"  28

P
Pan-Africanism  40, 48, 214
Parker, Pat  169
Parks, Rosa  134, 203
Partido Revolucionario de los Trabajadores (PRT)  168
Passive resistance  20, 20–21
People of color movements  170, 180–181, 191, 192
People's Antiwar Mobilization  176
People's front  120
Permanent Revolution  91, 102, 193, 194
Philadelphia, PA building trades protests  63, 208

Police brutality 142, 189
Powell, Adam Clayton 65, 208
Progressive Party 31
Pullman Company 117

**R**

Raab, Earl 185
Race as a social category 37–38,
   39
Race consciousness 40, 46, 50
"Race is primary" line 175
Racial discrimination 31
Racism 22, 38, 55, 92, 96, 124,
   146, 170, 174, 179, 180, 181,
   192
Radical organizations 51; and
   Black struggle 95–97, 134,
   141, 173
Radical Women (RW) 13, 165,
   168, 176, 181, 182, 197
Randolph, A. Phillip 116–118,
   149–150, 153, 205
Reagan, President Ronald 172–
   173, 189
Reconstruction 23, 26, 37, 42,
   48, 58
Reed, John 98
Republic of New Africa 186,
   187
Republican Party 133, 188
Revolution in the U.S. 27, 50,
   76, 87, 92, 124, 126, 131,
   188, 194, 196, 197
Revolutionary Integration 15, 83,
   91–95, 98, 100, 114, 124,
   127, 128, 130, 179, 181–182,
   187, 192, 196, 201; essential
   premises 11, 73, 92–93, 124
Revolutionary Marxist party, tasks
   of 20, 68–69, 83, 93, 100–
   101, 126, 198–199
Revolutionary Union Movement
   154
Revolutionary Workers League
   179–180, 190
Ringgold, Faith 163
Roberts, Dan 69, 123
Rockwell, George Lincoln 130
Roosevelt, President Franklin D.
   116, 117, 205, 209

Russian Revolution 33, 95
Rustin, Bayard 208

**S**

Saunders, Lois 69
Scottsboro Boys 106, 119–120
Scottsboro Defense Committee
   120
Seale, Bobby 142
Seattle Anti-Klan Network 181
Seattle Black Women's Network
   181
Segregation 16, 20, 22, 27, 31,
   37, 38–39, 42, 55, 56, 58, 92,
   137
Self-defense 24, 49, 142, 144,
   145, 146
Self-determination, right of
   nations to 34, 36, 52, 53–54,
   55, 74, 102, 103–104, 105;
   applied to Blacks 52, 54, 75,
   82, 88, 99, 105, 108, 110,
   111–112, 113, 114, 127, 131
Selma, AL voter registration drive
   151
Separatism 39, 53–56, 103–104,
   157–158, 206. See also Black
   nationalism/separatism
Sexism 155, 170, 174, 180, 181,
   192
Sharecroppers Union 112, 212
Simon, Jean 128
Slave trade 47
Slavery in the U.S. 37, 57
Socialism 61, 73, 86, 122, 164,
   192, 193, 194
"Socialism in One Country" 104
Socialist feminism 13, 164–166,
   171, 182, 192, 196, 201
Socialist Party 49, 96, 97, 111,
   116, 207
Socialist Workers Party (SWP)
   12, 15, 31, 33, 68–89, 107,
   111, 115, 123–124, 126–130,
   133, 141, 147, 190, 210, 211;
   condemnation of interracial
   relations in party 121;
   involvement in Black movement 12, 68–78, 84–85, 119,
   120–121, 210; Los Angeles

branch 123–124, 126, 128;
nationalist approach to Black
movement 34, 70, 113, 121,
124, 127, 129, 131, 132–133;
proposal for Revolutionary
Integrationist strategy 10, 12,
83–89, 128; resolutions on
Black movement 51, 69, 70,
73, 112–114, 121–123, 126,
127–133, 206, 210; Seattle
branch 12, 15, 91, 123, 126,
128; sexism in 128; trade
unionist approach to Black
movement 70–72
Southern Christian Leadership
Conference (SCLC) 136–137,
203, 213
Southern police state 15, 16, 17,
20–22, 26, 27, 29, 93, 128,
133, 137
Spartacist League 179–181
Stalin, Joseph 35, 50, 102, 104,
106, 207, 211
Stalin-Hitler pact 118
Stalinism/Stalinists 49, 50, 53,
104, 107, 116, 118, 174, 175,
207
Student Non-Violent Coordinating Committee (SNCC) 9, 16,
107, 136–142, 181, 184, 203
Swabeck, Arne 69, 108–109,
110, 126

**T**

Taft-Hartley Act 28, 62, 63, 205
Terrell, Mary Church 161
Third International. *See
Comintern*
Till, Emmett 30, 205
Trade Union Education League 98
Trade unions. *See Labor move-
ment*
Trend, The 174–175
Trotsky, Leon 99, 104, 107, 108,
111, 126, 130, 147, 193, 207,
210; on the Black struggle 51,
78–80, 86, 107–108, 112,
114–115; on the National
Question 35
Trotskyism 87, 111

Trotter, William Monroe 42, 206
Truman, President Harry 117
Truth, Sojourner 161
Tubman, Harriet 161
Twain, Mark 58

**U**

U.S. armed forces 116, 120
U.S. Congress 23, 41, 84, 150
Unionism. *See Labor movement*
United Auto Workers 154
United Workers Union - Indepen-
dent 181
Universal Negro Improvement
Association 43–44, 48
University of Mississippi
desegregation battle 24–25,
204

**V**

Vanguard role of most oppressed
99, 165, 198; of Black women
197; of Blacks 61, 73, 82, 86,
93, 100, 110, 114, 124, 179,
194
Vernon, Robert 58, 81, 85, 129
Voting Rights Act 151, 172

**W**

Walker, Alice 163
Walker, Edwin A. 23, 204
Wallace, Michele *158*, 162–163,
181, 184
Washington, Booker T. 42, 43,
48, 206
Watts, CA riots 140, 151–152,
204
White Citizens Council 20
"White European" syndrome
178–179
White supremacy 22, 39, 45, 82,
111, 130
White workers 38, 56, 61, 72,
81, 87, 88, 99, 100, 110, 124,
131, 134, 148, 154, 200;
southern 17, 22, 26–27, 112,
125, 154
Wilkins, Roy 25, 204
Williams, Robert 16, 17, 144–
147, 203, 210

Williams, Wayne  168
"Wilmington Ten"  190
Woman Question (strategy for
    women's liberation)  142, 174,
    179
Women  137, 160. *See also
    Black women*
Women of color  179
Women's Political Council  135
Women's movement  155, 160,
    180. *See also Feminism*
Workers Party  111, 207
Workers World Party  175–177
World War II  107, 118
Worthy, William  19, 67, 86, 209
Wright, Bobby  184, 185

## Y
Young, Andrew  135, 188, 213

## Z
Zetkin, Clara  *35*

# RADICAL WOMEN Publications